PR LESSONS LEARNED ALONG THE WAY

Strategies, Tips & Advice for
the Higher Ed and Nonprofit
Public Relations Professional

Marc C. Whitt

Published By:

cherrymoon
M   E   D   I   A

Lexington, KY - (859) 397-9821
www.cherrymoonmedia.com

For the Whitt family

My wife, Jennifer McGuire Whitt;
my children, Emily Marie & Mark Wayne Fields,
Elizabeth Anne & Christian Muncie,
and Jacob Robert Whitt;
my grandchildren, Annaleigh Jaymes & Aubrey Clay Fields;
my father and mother, Calvin L. (1928-2017) & Dora Spears
Whitt;
and my parents-by-marriage, Donald G. and Lois Faye Coots
McGuire.

And to the Presidents, Faculty & Staff, Alumni & Students of
University of Kentucky
Eastern Kentucky University
Campbellsville University
Georgetown College
University of the Cumberlands
who have taught me more than I can ever repay.

With Special Appreciation to my dear Friend and College
Journalism Buddy,
Don McNay (1959 – 2016),
who inspired me to write this book six years ago,
and to
Cherrymoon Media Publisher Adam Turner,
University Business and Former Editor Tim Goral,
University Business Senior Managing Editor Melissa Ezarik,
Caitlin Lukacs, Manager of Editorial Content, Council for
Advancement & Support of Education,
University of Kentucky Chief Photographer Mark
Cornelison, and
Editorial Assistants Jerry Wallace & Joan C. McKinney,
with special thanks to Jay Blanton, University of Kentucky
AVP/Chief Communications Officer,
for his encouragement and support.
I am most grateful to each of you.

And in loving memory of my brother, Robert E. (Bob) Whitt.

CONTENTS

FOREWORD

BY MELISSA EZARIK

SENIOR MANAGING EDITOR - *UNIVERSITY BUSINESS*

Throughout each day during my 15 years planning editorial content for *University Business* magazine, press releases and story pitches pop up in my inbox from a variety of higher ed institutions (and industry reps, too). In fact, I could realistically spend just about all day, every day crafting thoughtful responses, ranging from firm "no thanks" notes (typically with a brief explanation) and replies that seek more information, to the always well-received "yes, this story is a great fit for us!" Dozens of names fill my Outlook "from" field in any given week. While I've certainly developed relationships with higher ed communications folks over the years, I'll be honest: My mental list of campus contacts I can match with a particular college in an instant is pretty short.

One big reason for this is that few take the time to really find out what kinds of news and ideas we need to fill our pages and fulfill our mission. Few have segmented lists of local and national media contacts. (Sorry, I won't be able to make it to your "lunch and learn" on Thursday because it would take me 15 hours to drive to your campus, but thanks for the invite and for following up when I didn't RSVP the first time.) Few seem to realize that a ranking of 38 on a best colleges list is not going to win our attention, or that I'll jump at the chance for us to cover a trend because yours is the first college in your state (the whole state!) to take an action. We love hearing what's going on with our readers, but our goal is to provide insights and actionable advice for administrators in every corner of campus and virtually every campus nationwide. So we treasure the rare pitch about an emerging national trend that applies to just a handful of U.S. colleges, the pitch that not only notes this, but even drops the names of other colleges engaged in the activity with links to learn more.

Marc Whitt is on my shortlist of memorable campus PR pros—the rare contact who gets it. In one of my early years at UB, he reached out to my editor and me with the request to learn more about how we make decisions on coverage. But Marc isn't the kind of guy to keep such knowledge to himself. Would we be willing to have a conversation simultaneously with communications staffers from colleges and universities within driving distance of his own Kentucky campus so they could all gain perspective on how to successfully pitch UB?

Based in Connecticut, we realized we wouldn't be able travel to Marc, at Campbellsville University, for such a meeting. So he suggested a virtual meetup. Lacking any sophisticated technology on our end, this meant setting a laptop in the center of the conference room table, placing the office microwave's turntable under the laptop, and taking turns answering questions, adjusting the laptop as needed so the event attendees could see us. Marc had gathered a small but engaged audience, in his conference room. This maximized our time by allowing us to share how we work with many at once. The professionals, from a number of institutions in the vicinity, not only learned tips for pitching ideas to us, but also learned from Marc, the facilitator, about the kinds of questions to ask editors in the future.

Several years later, Marc began sharing his own expertise nationally as UB's marketing and PR columnist. Expanded versions of many of those columns—along with additional content derived from his 35 years of having served at church-related, public regional, and public land-grant colleges and universities, plus from his consulting work for various for-profit and nonprofit organizations—now appear in this collection.

Entry-level PR pros serving within higher ed and at nonprofits in other industries will see this as an accessible and personable guidebook. Reading Marc's experiences and advice will feel like sitting down with a mentor over a cup (many cups!) of coffee.

But midcareer and senior-level professionals will also find much to savor here. The wisdom and ideas found within these pages can help anyone glean guiding principles to support them through both great and not-so-great days.

All aspects of PR and marketing are touched upon, from advice on multitasking and harnessing the power of social media to tips on crisis communication, town and gown, and effective capital campaign messaging. The message: Know how to be tactical in communication, but aim for strategic.

Each chapter is divided by a page featuring a few "PR lessons learned along the way" that are intended to encourage, remind and challenge the reader. These browsable gems could fill their own inspirational quote book or vision board. For example: "Never give bad news more life than it deserves. Address it head-on with full transparency, honesty, and timeliness," or "Tear down organizational silos by implementing honest, civil, constructive communication. This will build walkways and bridges of trust and collaboration."

Marc shares campus experiences with obvious practicality as well as family stories, which he connects to effective work in the field. He absorbed lessons in exceptional customer service and reputational branding from his granddad, a service station owner. And his dad, who spent much of his career directing a high school band, taught devotion to the perfection of a craft and a passion for instruction. They're the sort of life lessons many of us have learned because of family or other mentors, and this book will encourage reflective thought on the people who shaped us—

and on how we can serve as mentors ourselves, helping others along on their journey to success.

Melissa Ezarik

Senior Managing Editor

University Business

"New PR is about people and relationships, not just new tools. The game is changing, and it's survival not only of the fittest, but also of the most capable and sincere."

-Brian Solis and Deirdre Breakenridge

Putting the Public Back in Public Relations

"

Never surprise the president.

"

The first piece of advice offered to me as a PR intern my junior year in college by then-Eastern Kentucky University President Dr. J.C. Powell.

Never give bad news more life than it deserves. Address it head-on with full transparency, honesty and timeliness.

"

Take time to understand the interests of media management, editors, news directors, reporters, writers and the audiences they serve. Then align your stories and pitches accordingly. This is the first step to effective media relations.

"

Make yourself indispensable.

CAREER AND LIFE LESSONS
LEARNED ALONG THE WAY
A PERSONAL REFLECTION

I have discovered that since reaching the age of 60, I have become much more reflective about my life and career. That doesn't mean, though, I'm slowing down by any means!

Perhaps I've become more reminiscent because I am entering a new chapter of life as a husband, dad, granddad ("Papa" to my grandchildren), son, uncle, citizen volunteer and, of course, a public relations and marketing professional who has devoted 35 years and counting to higher education and nonprofit causes.

Then again, maybe it's because I'm at a point in

my career where I receive mail from AARP and invitations to address conference and workshop sessions for "senior" or "seasoned" professionals! (When did *that* happen?)

Whatever the reason for that spirit of reflection, I enjoy being on this side of my career and watching an incredibly talented and gifted group of young professionals accept a calling into a career in higher education or nonprofit public relations or marketing.

Serving in this profession has been one of my life's great fulfillments. It has taken me to places and introduced me to people this Eastern Kentucky boy never imagined he would see or meet.

Through the people and experiences I have encountered along the way, I have been molded and shaped by a career filled with plenty of joys and some sorrows, many wins and a few defeats— all of which have made me the grateful and blessed public relations professional I am today.

At the onset of this book, permit me to be a bit opinionated. I, for one, believe those of us who have devoted our careers to the calling of public relations or marketing are *professionals*, not *practitioners*. And that is not merely arguing semantics. Professional communicators are *strategic* communicators. Practitioner communicators are *tactical* communicators.

Allow me to elaborate. When I was a student at Eastern Kentucky University studying the art and craft of public relations and communication, I became equipped to understand the basics of the work – the tactics. I quickly grasped what we all recognize to be the fundamental skills required of our work: writing, editing and disseminating news releases and media advisories, organizing special events and, of course, writing and designing publications.

Following graduation, I was then able to exercise these tactical skills daily when I accepted my first professional job overseeing church relations at what is now known as the University of the Cumberlands.

But as I evolved in the work, I found myself becoming much more engaged in planning, crafting and evaluating communication strategy. In time, my advice was sought and trusted by the college's senior leadership. Suffice it to say, this level of PR and marketing leadership demands incredible trust, responsibility and confidence from those you counsel. And none of this occurred overnight. It took a lot of hard work, patience, trial and error, faith and teamwork.

I was offering the best counsel I could at the time with the goal of best positioning or branding my institution and its leadership. This is when my metamorphosis took me from public relations and marketing *practitioner* to the next career stage – the *professional*.

Kirk Hazlett, a well-respected PR professional and longtime advocate of PRSA and PRSSA, perhaps said it best:

"'Practitioners,' to me, are those folks who have learned the tactics and techniques of the public relations 'business.' They are skilled writers. They are talented media relations experts. They are adept at taking the raw materials of a client's specialty area and turning them into communication tools that effectively promote that client's business.

They're the technicians who make sure that the nuts-and-bolts of the client's communication programs are up to snuff.

'Professionals,' on the other hand, do this and so much more. They also fully comprehend and embrace the nuances of our craft, and they are prepared with advice and counsel to steer the client through to success.

They are the pathfinders who share the client's vision and offer guidance that helps prepare in advance for situations that oftentimes have not yet bubbled to the surface."

So throughout this book, I will use the term *professional* rather than *practitioner* because today's highly competitive marketplace requires, if not demands, the higher education or nonprofit public relations or marketing professional to be a creative, big-thinking, problem-solving, can-do *strategic* communicator.

That said, one of the finest public relations and marketing mentors I ever had was my maternal grandfather, John Spears. (You'll read a bit about him in a later chapter. He was pretty amazing!)

Never once did he take a PR course or practice the profession. Never once did he attend a college class, although he used to enjoy saying that he "went through college" when taking my uncle or mom back to school at the start or close of each semester at Centre College. But the wisdom, joy and understanding of customer service was manifested in the way he managed his life, family and work. He exampled in so many ways lessons that I—and now you—can apply to our personal and professional lives.

For nearly 35 years he owned and operated a Pure Oil service station (later a Union76) in my hometown of Paintsville, Kentucky, population 3,500 and located in the heart of Appalachia

Kentucky.

For those 30 or younger, this period in America's history was before self-serve gas pumps were the rage and eventually became commonplace. Back in those "good old days," it was no accident that the word "service" appeared before "station" – *service* always came first.

My granddad's service station was a handsomely designed, cottage-like building that often received awards from the local garden club. It was located in the middle of a busy small-town business district. If you were driving through town or walking to a department store or bank, or grabbing a quick burger and fries at one of the nearby restaurants, you had to pass by "Johnny Spears' station."

It was a hub of activity—comparable in many ways to Andy Griffith's famed TV town of Mayberry and its courthouse and jail.

Even though my Granddad Spears (whom we called "Zoom" because the Pure Oil firebird "zoomed" and the name stuck) died many years ago, his reputation as an honest, hardworking, wise, steady businessman is nearly legendary in my hometown.

Along with a full tank of gas and an ice-capped, 6 ½-ounce bottle of Coca-Cola, customers came to expect an encouraging word and above-the-call-of-duty service.

That exemplary service became my granddad's "brand." His customers pulled in for excellent service and drove away receiving an exceptional experience. It was customer service at its finest, and the word-of-mouth marketing he and his service station earned surpassed his need to ever advertise in the local newspaper or on our town's radio station.

I was fortunate to work for him during the summers while I was in high school. More than learning the proper way to change a car's oil and spark plugs or perform a wash-and-wax job without leaving towel streaks, my granddad taught me through word and deed some of the greatest public relations and marketing lessons I've ever learned in or out of the classroom.

The attention to customer service and commitment to excellence have remained with me throughout my career. Here are a few but important lessons he taught those of us who knew and loved him:

- Meet each day with expectation of making a difference for your business and customers.

- A smile is much easier to wear than a frown.

- Don't argue with the customer. It's not that his or her complaint is necessarily right, but it is far better to seek resolution than send them on their way dissatisfied.

- Customers expect excellent service. They will remember and tell their friends when it is exceptional.

- Your "brand" is your reputation and, good or bad, will travel by word of mouth among your current and potential customers.

- Be responsive to your customers in a timely manner.

- Believe in your product or service and market it with enthusiasm and sincerity.

What wonderful PR and marketing lessons these were – *and are*!

Whether you are an entry-level, mid-career or senior professional at a college, university or nonprofit organization, these guiding principles can lead and support you through many great and some not-so-great days.

In the spirit of growing together in this profession, I offer you a few of my observations— life lessons, if you will—that are relevant no matter the stage of your career.

Many in today's business world often refer to these lessons as "soft skills." I, on the other hand, contend that they are *not* soft, but should be regarded as *essential* or *indispensable* career skills, especially for those of us who serve in the relationship-building fields of public relations and marketing.

For most of you, the lessons I've learned along my journey merely confirm the many good works you have accomplished throughout your career.

You are successful because you have devoted yourself to quality, excellence, loyalty, lifelong learning and seizing both large and small opportunities whenever they have presented themselves.

For others who are relatively new to the field, these lessons learned are intended to help keep you on the road to success while avoiding as much as possible the unforeseen pitfalls that can end in a PR or marketing faux pas or worse – a disaster.

Lesson #1: Keep Yourself Fresh and Relevant in the Profession

Henry Ford, American industrialist and founder of the Ford Motor Company, said, "Anyone who stops learning is old, whether at twenty or eighty. Anyone who keeps learning stays young."

Appreciating and dedicating yourself to lifelong learning is critical if you intend to remain razor-sharp throughout your career. The process does not end when you earn that college degree. Quite frankly, it's just beginning!

It is imperative more than ever that today's public relations and marketing professionals keep actively involved in at least one professional organization such as the Public Relations Society of America, Council for Advancement and Support of Education and American Marketing Association, Public Relations and Communications Association or the Chartered Institute of Public Relations, a professional body in the United Kingdom for public relations professionals. You may wish to consider several others, as this is just a sampling of worthy professional organizations.

Membership and involvement will help you become a better, more productive professional as you will keep abreast of the latest trends and developments in our profession, not to mention the incredible networking opportunities such memberships afford.

Often I have consulted with or offered counsel to peers facing a new challenge or opportunity. Involvement with at least one professional organization can encourage dialogue, sharing of ideas and promotion of collaboration among peers.

Remaining fresh in the work requires the seasoned professional of 10 or more years to keep up with the latest in technologies and communication advances. The days of solely depending on a brochure, newsletter, advertisement or well-placed news release to tell your organization's story are long gone.

For Millennials or Gen Z'ers, such as my three children who grew up in the Digital Age (also known as the Information Age), communication technologies such as texting, instant messaging and FaceTiming, as well as posting statuses, stories, photos and tweets on numerous social media platforms like Facebook, Twitter, LinkedIn, YouTube, Instagram, Skype, SnapChat, Pinterest and nearly 100 others are no big deal. It's as much second nature for them as it was for a Baby Boomer like me to twist the dial on a television set or dial what is now called on Amazon a "vintage rotary dial telephone."

Just recently, I witnessed my nearly 3-year old granddaughter holding an iPad and swiping the screen until she landed on the program she wanted to watch! I was amazed! This activity was nothing for her! It was second nature. For those of you with young children or grandchildren, you know what I mean! Very young children are quickly adapting communication technologies it has taken older folks like me to learn – and it's exciting to watch.

Whether you like it or not, the evolution of social media, mobile technologies and the Internet is here to stay and will undoubtedly expand our understanding of the world around us – both good and bad. Communication technology has reduced the size of our world by granting us countless opportunities to share and network with one another. Despite its critics, I'm excited to be living in a time to *see* and *use* this technology!

Baby Boomers like me, we have two choices: we can either jump on the Digital Age Bandwagon enthusiastically by engaging ourselves in the emerging communication technologies and integrating them into our work or naively pretend all this Internet "stuff" is just a fad and will eventually go away.

The latter choice most certainly will lead to disastrous consequences for you and the organization you represent. Our organizations have every right to expect from their marketing and public relations officers a mastery of skills, as I'm sure you agree. This skillset includes personal engagement not only with the traditional tools of the trade, but with social media, mobile technologies and the Internet as well.

Not since the world's move from tapping out messages via Morse code to making scratchy sounding telephone calls thanks to Mr. Graham Bell's invention have we witnessed such awe-inspiring advances in communication technologies.

Last, but certainly not least, I firmly believe in the power of reading. One of the ways I continue to keep myself fresh in the profession is teaching an evening class or two – something I have done for approximately 25 years and currently do in the Department of Integrated Strategic Communication at the University of Kentucky.

Serving as a part-time instructor has made me a better public relations and marketing professional. I realize teaching isn't everyone's cup of tea. But for me, it has challenged me to read and study more of the contemporary literature in public relations, communication studies, marketing and leadership. The enjoyment of not only reading the latest works in our profession but other topics that interest me help keep me relevant in my work while not depending on out-of-date strategies, theories or practices.

Teaching also has enabled me to be a better listener and observer with many of the thoughts, ideas and issues our students and faculty have. As a result, I can better understand a wide variety of viewpoints, communication styles and creative approaches – all of which make me a more effective public relations officer and hopefully a better person, friend, colleague and instructor.

I encourage those who are entering the profession or who, like me, have been around for a while to commit yourselves to lifelong learning. The older I get, the more I discover how much more I need to learn. Hunger for knowledge and understanding so that you may better serve others.

One last point I wish to make before we move on is that we must all learn how to face and accept the winds of change when they blow our way. Like death and taxes, change will inevitably affect us one way or another – directly or indirectly.

A friend of mine once told me she didn't mind change as long as it didn't affect her. We probably all feel that way at times, don't we?

In her book, *Let's Close A Deal*, award-winning author and speaker Christine Clifford said: "We never know which way the wind is going to blow in our careers. We can let it knock us off balance, or we can adjust our sails, put out our spinnaker and have the wind at our back propelling us along."

It doesn't take long to realize life is like one long rollercoaster that includes ups and downs, sharp banks, butterflies-in-the-stomach moments, barrel rolls, double-down drops and occasional bunny hops before the ride straightens up and slows down as we eventually roll into retirement. We all experience thrills, chills and a few occasional spills.

Our professional career's ride in public relations or marketing is much the same way as we experience and face whatever changes come our way.

Lesson #2: Seek a Mentor/Become a Mentor

Looking back over my career brings to mind so many people who have helped mold and shape me to become the public relations and marketing professional I am today. Most of us would agree that had it not been for those mentors along the way who opened doors of opportunity for us, our lives—both personally and professionally—would not be where they are.

"If I have seen further, it is by standing on the shoulders of giants," wrote Sir Isaac Newton.

I am a firm believer in mentoring. Had it not been for people who stepped up without hesitation to mentor me—to give me a chance to succeed or fail—I'm not sure where I would be today. In many ways, I am who I am because of the sacrifice of time, energy, care and concern shown me by my family, friends, teachers, neighbors, church, colleagues, peers, work and the good and not-so-good personal experiences along the way.

For those entering the field, it is vitally important that you seek out someone whose wise counsel and years of professional development will help mold and shape you into the professional you seek to become.

Much like the apprenticeship system first developed in the latter Middle Ages, mentoring places the curious student with the skilled teacher to learn his or her craft—in this case, public relations or marketing.

When you find that unique individual who becomes your mentor, observe all aspects of his or her professionalism. Pay special attention to your mentor's carefully-honed skills in listening, persuasion, small group interaction, crisis management and conflict resolution, and interpersonal communication, as well as her or his ability to enhance work atmospheres that encourage creativity, innovation, brainstorming, a passion and enthusiasm for the marketing and public relations craft, and a critical eye for detail.

Like a Middle Age apprenticeship, the teacher-mentor carefully and thoughtfully passes along to their student-mentee principles that will help establish a firm foundation that will carry them for the remainder of their careers.

I can never repay the debt I owe my earliest career mentors—people such as longtime University of Kentucky PR guru Bernie Vonderheide and higher education marketing legends Larry Lauer, Robert Topor and Bob Sevier; college and university presidents Drs. James H. Taylor (University of the Cumberlands), W Morgan Patterson (Georgetown College), Ken Winters (Campbellsville University), E. Bruce Heilman (University of Richmond) and Charles Doug Whitlock (Eastern Kentucky University); college and university advancement vice presidents J. Richard Carlton (Georgetown College), D. Michael Richey (University of Kentucky), Mary Kay Murphy (Oglethorpe University), Joan Bahner

(Fisk University) and Bart Meyer (EKU and UK); and EKU professors Robert Hartwell, David Greenlee, Max Huss and Dan Robinette.

Not only did these individuals rise to the highest heights of their chosen professions in higher education administration, teaching and advancement, they always made themselves available for a very green PR guy's questions, thoughts and occasional anxieties while assuring, challenging and encouraging me along the way. Despite the busyness of their schedules, they *always* gave me ample time.

For several of you, these people are familiar names. Like me, you found them to be valuable, trusted mentors. However, for several others of you reading this book, these names may be unfamiliar.

So why is it important that I list them here? First, this book provides me a unique opportunity to recognize and thank them, even though a few have since passed away. Secondly, I do so as a homework assignment for you.

I want you to put down this book for a few minutes, sip your coffee and think for a moment about those who, like these incredible men and women who impacted my life, mentored you. Who are they?

Have you ever taken the time to write down their names and follow-up with a "thank you" note, email, call or better yet, a personal visit? Don't wait to do this. Do it now.

I guarantee you this will be an important exercise for both you and your mentors. Your gratitude will most certainly bless their hearts – as we like to say in the South! It will also remind you that none of us, including you, would be where we are in our careers had it not been for the love, counsel, support and perhaps sacrifice one or more made for us along the way in our professional career's journey. We are truly blessed to have such mentors in our lives.

My mentors' spirit of servant leadership taught

me early in my career that if they were willing to mentor me as a very green college public relations and marketing pup, I someday would be in a position to do the same for others entering the profession. That *some day* has now become *today* for me.

Much of the genesis behind this book is the responsibility I feel as a senior professional to be a mentor for the new generation of higher education and nonprofit public relations and marketing professionals. It's my hope and sincere desire that something shared in the pages of this book will mentor the young professional, challenge the mid-career professional and encourage the senior professional.

Mentoring is a cyclical process. As a mentee, you should seek the best counsel you can get. When you have benefitted from that mentoring and added your acquired years of experience, you then as a professional marketer have the responsibility, perhaps an obligation, to pass on your art and craft to the next generation. And the cycle of mentoring continues.

In many ways, mentoring is paying tribute to those who made a difference in your early career while preparing the way for young professionals. For the young professional, seek out the best mentor you can find—one on whose shoulders you can stand. Before becoming that individual's mentee, carefully observe the quality of their character, integrity and core values.

After you find someone with these attributes, privately say to yourself: "I want to be like _____ ." From there, find ways you can observe and learn from this person. A vibrant, productive mentee/mentor relationship can become one of the most valuable treasures you'll obtain throughout your career – I promise you.

For the senior professional, make time to mentor. You have an obligation to the profession as well as to those who helped you become successful along the way. Regardless of how busy you may be, there is always time to mentor. The difference you can make in a young professional's career will far exceed your lifetime.

Lesson #3: Remember an Organization's Brand is Spelled "S-E-R-V-I-C-E"

Noted marketing consultant and author Harry Beckwith stands among the marketing authorities who argue that an organization's brand is much more than its logo, color scheme or tagline. An organization's brand is about the service it delivers to the customer and how it will be remembered—good or bad.

I first met Harry at a conference I helped organize more than 15 years ago. Upon hearing his address based on his best-selling book, *Selling the Invisible*, I was so impressed that I wrote it down for future reference: "In the public's eye, a brand is a warranty. It is a promise that the service carrying that brand will live up to its name, and perform." So often, nonprofit organizations get caught up in what I call "Tagline Paralysis" or

"Logo-itis." An organization's senior officers labor hours upon hours to come up with a catchy tagline or eye-popping logo—neither of which is necessarily wrong if properly given the right perspective.

That time spent is wrong, however, when we forget that an organization's brand is developed more authentically by how well we deliver our promise to the customer. No matter how attractive your logo might be or how creatively snappy your advertising tagline might sound, the customer is more inclined to remember how well your organization has treated him or her and whether he or she received what you promised.

Harry Beckwith, as I previously said, calls it a "warranty with the customer."

Please don't misunderstand me. I am a huge proponent of graphic and message consistency. In my earlier career, I once oversaw the protection and management of our institutional marks, colors and tagline. Too many organizations devote an excessive amount of attention to promoting the graphic identification side of corporate branding and far less on customer service. I contend we should flip the order to achieve a more accurate, more positive brand for our organizations. I have found that when customers are pleased by the service they receive, the graphic identifiers reinforce the organization's positive image.

Whenever customers believe they have been treated with utmost respect and attention, and have had their problem or issue solved, their branding image of us will catch on like a wildfire, a phenomenon that we in the marketing community call "word-of-mouth," or viral, marketing. A satisfied customer is the best marketing strategy of all!

Customers come to us expecting excellence. They remember and tell their friends when they have received exceptional service. Be exceptional.

Lesson #4: Start Strong. Finish Stronger!

Early in my career, I was asked to assist with the

marketing of a capital campaign. The concept for this particular effort was rather innovative. Rather than initiating a more traditional model in which a single college would be the sole beneficiary of philanthropic support, this campaign would establish a collaboration of three sister colleges that envisioned a rare and extraordinary effort to raise several millions of dollars from among their current and prospective donor pools.

The campaign, they thought, would attract more significant support than any one institution could achieve through its fundraising efforts. Besides, the donors would appreciate how their dollars could benefit the greater good of the three.

Just like the Three Musketeers, "All for one and one for all!" was the campaign's underlying mantra.

The idea seemed simple enough. Who wouldn't appreciate three competing sister colleges joining forces to raise much-needed funds for student scholarships and capital improvements?

Collaboration made perfect sense and appealed well to alumni and friends of the schools alike.

The capital campaign also shared additional pluses: 1) the relatively short-staffed development operations would be tripled in size, thus allowing for a more concentrated and effective fundraising effort; and 2) the launching of a comprehensive marketing campaign to initiate the capital campaign's awareness phase would most certainly raise awareness and visibility of the colleges throughout the state.

Everything seemed perfect. Before the capital campaign's launch, the energy among the leadership team was electric. The campaign logo was designed and approved. The creative and media placement for a series of testimonial print ads were ready to roll as were a set of handsomely designed direct-mail publications that touted the capital campaign's goals, benefits and timelines.

After weeks of preparation and countless leadership team meetings, the Big Day had arrived for the three presidents to announce the launch of the capital campaign. Again, everything appeared to be in place: a well-suited room for a news conference, an excellent turnout of college trustees and current donors, and a press contingency that would make even the White House press secretary proud!

What, you might ask, could go wrong? Unfortunately, what could have become a national model for collaboration wound up falling flat.

After all the hoopla had died down, the tedious work began in earnest to raise the much-anticipated millions of dollars. What started as a noble effort soon became an embarrassment for the colleges as current and prospective donors decided their institutional loyalties far outweighed the common good for all three.

The marketing campaign, initially funded jointly by the institutions, also suffered. Despite its well-defined goals, objectives and timelines, the leadership team's initial commitment slowly dwindled, and, as a result, the proverbial air leaked from the capital campaign's tires.

The moral of this story is simple. Often campaigns begin actively with much energy, support, enthusiasm, attention and expectation. Occasionally, the lifeblood for that energy, support and enthusiasm begins to wane for one reason or another, and, after a few days or weeks, the once well-intended effort falls short of its goal or dies for lack of interest and support.

Recently I watched a persuasive commercial for a nonprofit organization that asked viewers to join in its effort to conquer a particular societal ill. I was convinced and immediately went to the website and provided my name and contact information. I wanted to join the cause!

That was a year ago, and I have yet to receive a response to my inquiry! Even though the cause began strong, it finished weakly.

This anecdote is not intended to be a criticism for the 95 percent of the nonprofit organizations that do a superior job with their marketing and public relations initiatives. Hats off to you for the marvelous causes you represent and for the well-executed marketing communications plans you manage.

I do believe, however, there's a good reminder for each of us. It is absolutely critical that we begin strong and finish even stronger. When we do, our organizations and our supporters will truly be the beneficiaries of our care, planning and execution. Success truly breeds success.

Lesson #5: Your Name is All You Really Own. Protect It!

As the last lesson I wish to present, please close your office door or find a place of privacy.

Once you have done so, please find a blank sheet of paper. Draw a line down the center of the page. At the top of the left column, write: "Characteristics of Integrity." On the opposite side, now write: "Characteristics without Integrity."

Give yourself about 30 minutes to do this exercise. Don't take phone calls. Don't check your texts or emails. Don't be distracted. Simply think about people you know who exemplify either characteristic. What do they have in common? What do you like or dislike about their qualities? If you were shipwrecked on a deserted island, would you want them with you?

Now be brutally honest with yourself. Which column do you resemble the most?

No matter what profession or life direction you choose, your integrity will be challenged and when that happens, how will you respond?

This brings me to the point about integrity in your career. Much has been said or written about integrity during the past several years.

Albert Einstein said, "Whoever is careless with the truth in small matters cannot be trusted with important matters."

Oprah Winfrey said, "Real integrity is doing the right thing, knowing that nobody's going to know

47

whether you did it or not."

One of my favorite quotes about integrity is attributed to Warren Buffett. "Somebody once said that in looking for people to hire, you look for three qualities: integrity, intelligence, and energy," Buffet said. "And if you don't have the first, the other two will kill you."

As one who is engaged in public relations or marketing, you have been given much freedom to perform your duties. You will meet with numerous people from countless walks of life during your career. You often will be faced with making difficult decisions or resolving serious issues or conflicts. These are a few of the aspects of public relations that have blessed my life these past 35 years.

I am an immeasurably blessed person for having chosen this profession. I hope I have and continue to serve it well.

At times, though, you may be encouraged by a colleague or client to turn your head the other way.

"No one will notice," they argue. "What difference will it make?"

We have all faced making a decision that could either support or destroy our integrity. When those moments happen—and they will!—remember that you only have one name that has been given to you. Always seek what is honest and just. Apply these precepts to your decision making, and your name will forever be respected among your peers and colleagues as integrity always matters, whether it be in marketing, public relations, fundraising, accounting, teaching or any other profession.

Summary

My dad, who has since passed away, spent much of his career as a high school band director. Throughout his tenure, I witnessed firsthand his love and devotion to the perfection of his musical craft and passion for teaching.

Dad passed on to my brother and me that same burning desire to appreciate the art of music, and to this day, I continue to play trumpet and am joined by my wife, two daughters, son, and mother in playing a musical instrument. I suppose you can say it's our way of keeping family harmony!

You may say, "That's nice, but what do PR and marketing have to do with your dad being a band director?"

Actually, what I learned from him illustrates several points for which you may apply to your work in marketing and public relations:

• **Practice makes perfect.** No one ever begins our profession knowing everything. Practicing your skill and craft is essential to becoming the seasoned professional colleagues and clients will one day seek and respect.

• **Be passionate about your calling.** Allow a fire of enthusiasm and inquisitiveness to burn in you. Others will be attracted to you.

• **See to the details.** Similar to a sheet of music that calls for measures of loud and soft passages, the slightest of details will be noticed by the audience, and they will remember you for that.

• Playing in the band calls for teamwork. Regardless of how talented you are, PR and marketing still take, like being in the band, a dedicated team to create something much larger than yourself. Be team-oriented and seek counsel from those inside and outside the field.

• Lastly, be ready for the performance. When the time comes for you to take those hours of review and practice to the public, make sure you start strong and finish even stronger. Your organization will thrive and your audience will rave with glowing reviews. Bravo!

I would be remiss if I didn't mention one of the most crucial PR lessons I've learned along the way: the art and skill of listening, which has been taught and exampled to me by several women in my life – particularly my wise and loving wife and mom, and Mary Kay Murphy and Joan Bahner, who I already mentioned.

How much we need to learn and adopt the

ability to listen twice as much as we enjoy talking. We miss out on so much when we do not genuinely listen to the other person – especially when their perspective may not jibe with ours.

These ladies' ability to be truly excellent listeners has not gone unnoticed or appreciated by their family, friends and colleagues. They put away all distractions—including smartphones (!)—so that they may focus their full attention on the one with whom they are conversing.

We all need to practice better listening skills. Imagine how much more we could learn from one another if we merely *listened*! It's the first step toward effective communication!

In his 20th James C. Bowling Executive-In-Residence Lecture sponsored by the University of Kentucky Department of Integrated Strategic Communication and the UK Journalism and Media Alumni Association, Roger Bolton, president of Page, said of listening:

"When we do … listening well, we encourage the

organization to embrace diversity. This has the dual benefit of being the right thing to do, because it gives opportunities to diverse populations, and also of being good for the institution, because it enables it to make better decisions, informed by a wider range of relevant facts, and to build broader public support."

Later in his remarkable address before a standing-room-only audience of communication students, faculty and administrators, Bolton said:

"If we want to be good persuaders, we also must be willing to be persuaded. Organizations that listen well are the best at building relationships of trust based on shared belief. Too often in the past the practice of public relations stops with belief. We want people to understand our point of view. To accept it. To think well of us and our brand. But this is actually just the beginning of the journey, not the end. When done well, building shared belief can lead to positive actions by stakeholders, such as buying products, investing in the company, entering into partnerships and the like. Over time, as stakeholder relationships deepen, they can lead to mutual confidence and respect (that is, a strong

and positive reputation) that may result in advocacy by stakeholders."

I now invite you to join me through the pages of this book of career lessons I have learned along the way. And by the time you reach the final page, I hope there has been something written that will inspire, encourage, make you think or even question. If this has been achieved, we both succeed!

Now, go warm up that cup of coffee and let's begin this journey together.

"

Never burn a bridge. Never.
Ever.

"

"

Listen five times more than you talk. You'll be amazed by what you learn.

Public Relations is more about working behind the scenes than being on the stage.

"

Remember to maintain close relations with the community that hosts your institution. The citizenry and civic leaders are among your best supporters. Communicate with them. Engage them. Seek innovative partnerships.

ADVICE FOR THE FIRST-TIME COLLEGE MARKETING OFFICER

FIVE WAYS TO MAKE YOUR JOURNEY A SMOOTH ONE

Congratulations, you've landed your first job as a college's chief public relations and marketing officer. It's a grand role loaded with ocean-size opportunities and responsibilities.

I got my first director's position in 1988 when I joined the staff at Georgetown College in Kentucky. Up until then I had been a one-person shop.

With my appointment at Georgetown, I found myself managing a four-person staff, a budget and the institution's external and internal relations, while seeking to build on a communication foundation established by my predecessor.

The immensity of the role didn't hit me until the vice president handed me the keys to my office and said, "Well, Marc, it's all yours."

As you launch into your new journey, I encourage you to adopt five practices that are just as applicable for the CCO or CMO who has recently moved from another institution into this role.

Expect failure

No matter how talented, creative, articulate and smart you are, there will be times when your idea crashes and burns, you've been misquoted by the media or the event you plan attracts only members of your immediate family.

Don't allow an occasional failure to topple your world. We've all been there. But experiencing times of failure actually grows and strengthens us as we develop as professionals. American businessman Sumner Redstone said: "Success is not built on success. It's built on failure. It's built on frustration. Sometimes it's built on catastrophe."

Learn and respect the culture of your environment

Each institution has its own character and set of values and traditions. Become a sponge. Allow yourself to be absorbed by your institution's culture.

Learn all you can about its history, its legends, its victories and times of sacrifice

Discover its unique qualities. Listen to your president, administrative leadership, and current and retired members of the faculty and staff.

Understand your institution's town-gown relations and connections with the region it serves. By doing so, the campus community will more quickly trust in you as a person and leader.

Plan your work, and work your plan

Leading a college's public relations and marketing program is a big job that comes with plenty of responsibilities. You cannot afford to shoot from the hip.

If the administration hasn't already done so, develop in collaboration with your president and vice president no more than five goals to achieve within your first and second years. A good plan will establish a road map for you to follow and will protect you from wandering in the wilderness guessing where to step next.

Effective planning provides you with direction and demonstrates mature leadership.

Build and maintain productive relationships

We are in the relationship business. Balance your social and digital media efforts with time spent face-to-face with constituents on and off-campus.

For those new public relations and marketing professionals who can balance and master both, the world will be yours. Become a familiar face on your campus and in the community.

Enjoy frequent conversations with members of

your faculty and staff, and with civic leaders. Be a smart, strategic networker who builds personal relationships, and who strives to establish connections with the institution you serve.

Secure a mentor

Lastly, find someone you trust, perhaps a former college professor or a peer at another institution, who is willing to mentor you. We all need someone who can provide sage counsel should we face a sensitive issue or a crisis situation on campus.

A seasoned professional who can offer you their ear, shoulder and words of wisdom will be a tremendous asset as you move into this wonderful profession so many of us cherish.

(An updated and expanded version of a story originally published in *University Business*. Used by permission.)

"

An elementary teacher once
asked her class to define the
word 'Salt.' Thinking a bit, the
student responded: 'Salt is what
you don't notice unless it's
missing.' PR is much the same
way.

"

"

Meet each day with high expectations. Seek to make a measured difference for your organization and its supporters.

"

"

Remind yourself that even on tough, trying days, you're blessed to be doing what you're doing.

"

"

Timing is everything. Great ideas have crashed because the timing of their launch was not properly strategized.

"

Balancing Act

How to keep the plates from falling — and other strategies for managing the PR office

As a little boy, I watched "The Ed Sullivan Show" on TV every Sunday night at eight o'clock. *(For Millennials and Gen Zers who might be unfamiliar with "The Ed Sullivan Show," it was America's longest-running variety show, which aired on CBS from 1948 to 1971.)*

One act, in particular, sticks out in my mind.

Often on the popular variety program, showman Erich Brenn would come out on stage and spin a dinner plate on top of a stick. He'd then fly down to the other end of the stage to spin another dish. Then he'd rush to the center and whirl yet another one. By the time his act was in full swing, Brenn would be working feverishly to keep six plates from slowing down and crashing to the floor.

Our jobs in public relations and marketing are much the same way, aren't they? If you're like me and work in a college or university public relations shop, you know what it's like to keep your many plates spinning without letting a single one crash.

Maybe today's plate is the report the president's office must have within 15 minutes. Maybe it's the news conference you're running the same day you send your alumni magazine to the printer. Or perhaps it's a crisis you must help your campus leaders manage.

Juggling all of these and so many other pressing tasks can prove monumental. But whether you have several staff members or you're the one person who's all things to all people, you can keep your act going. As the following eight principles show, all you need is steadiness, smarts – and just the right amount of spin.

Plan well

Located in Kentucky, Mammoth Cave is the longest-known cave system in the world. When the tour guide takes you inside, the total darkness overwhelms you – that is, until the guide lights the torch. The flame rivets everyone's attention and your tour can proceed.

Likewise, unless you have a solid plan for your public relations program, you might as well be walking around in a dark cave.

Each year many PR and marketing offices set goals for their news, print and digital communications, marketing, sports information and community relations efforts. These goals, approved and supported by the administration, further all of our institutions' missions.

To keep staff from going helter-skelter, the best-managed offices will typically meet as a unit at least once a week if not more to discuss the current affairs of the college or university and focus on the most critical tasks. These meetings also allow the staff to use this time as a planning session so that they are prepared for future opportunities or challenges.

Such meetings may take time away from your hectic schedule. But don't allow the "I'm too busy working to plan" excuse to rule you. Without proper planning and productive communication with your staff, you as their manager, and your direct reports will be forever in the dark.

Be a strategist

PR directors are often relegated to overseeing the tactical objectives of our work: writing news releases, designing print and digital communications, planning special events, preparing the alumni magazine and so forth. We excel at performing such tasks.

Today's chief public relations officer must not only excel as overseeing such tactical objectives, but must be at "the table" of developing institutional policies and planning – in other words, becoming a strategic communicator.

Test yourself to see which you are: a tactical or strategic communicator.

When an unfortunate matter occurs, does your president ask you to recommend ways to handle the matter? When a rift takes place between your institution and the community or a neighborhood, do administrators put you in charge of healing the wounds? If another department is preparing a print or digital communication, does it come to you for ideas on purpose, content and design? When the institution's strategic plan is in the discussion and planning stages, is your input sought?

If you can answer yes to these questions, the higher-ups view you and your office as a viable source for strategic advice. If you answer no, you need to evaluate your status with key decision makers – and change it.

Start by proving to them that your level of training and experience can benefit your institution. They'll be more likely to ask your advice if you demonstrate maturity, creativity, dependability, level-headedness and strong management and communication skills.

To demonstrate that you possess these important qualities, work closely with your president. Let him or her see you often – and see you as a strategist, a planner, a keen and thoughtful observer who is trustworthy and can maintain confidences.

Several years ago, I had an opportunity to consult an outstanding liberal arts college. The president, eager to have his college's PR and marketing program moving forward, claimed that he hadn't heard from his chief PR officer in three weeks! That kind of visibility—or lack thereof—will not lead to greater appreciation for you and your staff.

Search for creative ideas

The economist Henry George once said, "There is danger in reckless change, but greater danger in blind conservatism."

The moral for PR officers: You have to take risks to make progress. Though time is tight and it's easier to do things the way you've always done them, resist the temptation to settle for the first solution that comes to mind. Stir your creative juices. Let your mind go.

What kind of free thinking can help you? How often do you employ the use of the PR "war room" with your staff and others when seeking creative answers and directions?

Choose quality over quantity

I am always amused by some PR officers who are quick to point out the number of news releases they write each year. Who cares? Unless the media are picking up a high percentage of those releases (or pitches) in whole or part, it's meaningless to mass-produce them. The only thing this accomplishes is to waste time you're already short on.

Instead, what counts is the quality of your work

— and what it accomplishes. Whether you're preparing a feature story, a recruitment brochure or an ad, gear it toward a specific target group with a specific result in mind.

Stretch your staff

The added power of students can boost today's public relations office. Communication students through internships and workstudy can provide any size PR operation with valuable assistance with writing stories, taking photos, assisting with social media, providing clerical support and much more.

This added workforce allows the director and staff to oversee more pressing matters while granting students meaningful, real-world work experiences before they graduate.

Finding trustworthy and talented students for such assignments is critical. Coming to work on time, meeting several deadlines a day and holding certain confidences can prove challenging for even the best and brightest students.

I often hear how colleges and universities across

the nation are able to attract such students by appealing to their interest to tell their institution's story in creative ways and by giving them a leg-up in a highly competitive marketplace for top communication graduates.

One example of how students can help you along these lines in with the preparation and release of hometown news releases. The media of your students' hometowns are always interested in how Johnny or Susie are doing; thanks to your novice newswriters, photographers, videographers and social media marketers, you'll soon reap even more exposure for your college or university.

Develop productive media relations

I attended a conference a few years ago where a panel of PR directors asked a panel of journalists what types of news they wanted. Most of their suggestions leaned toward what research institutions can offer: health news, medical breakthroughs and so on.

A small-college PR director, obviously

aggravated, threw up his arms in desperation and exclaimed, "I guess my campus's news is unimportant!"

Nonsense!

Never, ever forget this: Every, and I mean EVERY, institution, large or small, regardless of mission, has a story to tell and a purpose to fill. After all, a good story is a good story no matter from where it comes. Period.

Each of us has extraordinary stories to tell. The trick is in deciding which ones to pitch and how.

Because you can't make that decision in a vacuum, you must take time to know reporters, news directors, editors, general managers, publishers, assignment editors, photographers, videographers and producers, and for them, to get to know you as well.

Since most of us are trying for local, regional or statewide coverage, this is easy enough: Make strategic appointments with key media representatives. Then sit down and talk about what they want to cover and how news, faculty experts and events might match their interests.

Don't waste reporters' time with a story only a few people would find interesting such as staff promotions or small gifts and grants. Instead, discuss the contributions your faculty and staff are making to your community, region or state. Offer human-interest stories about alumni and students. Or faculty experts who can speak on current, newsworthy issues such as medical breakthroughs, environmental protection, drug awareness, workforce development, education and the impact of worldwide conflicts on international students, to name but a few.

Advice from others

You may know the saying, "The more, the merrier." Although you need to be careful not to sign over your office to amateurs, allowing others to take part in your program can give you new perspectives and ideas that only those not in PR can offer.

One way to do that is developing an advisory council of community leaders who will truly support your efforts. The better they understand your role, the better your program will be.

An advisory council can come in various forms. It may be a separate group or a committee of an already-existing organization. Such groups are especially useful at small colleges and universities or nonprofit organizations.

At a private university where I once served, we had a Public Relations Committee of the Board of Advisors. The advisory board and this committee met twice during the academic year and included members who were represented print and broadcast media organizations. They became some of that institution's more effective advocates across the region and state.

Granted, this type of advisory group might not work for you and your institution. But if you believe it might, make sure to provide members with a job description that will make their time, creativity and energies worth their efforts and yours.

Last but not least, try to anticipate everything

One complaint I often hear from PR offices is "I (We) don't have time to do it all."

They're always behind the eight ball – and as a result, they do few things on time and fewer things well.

What they're forgetting is that *everyone* is short on time – even folks with PR operations 10 times the size of small shops. There's no excuse for incompetence. If we're behind the eight ball, it's up to us—and only us—to get out.

So think ahead. Anticipate deadlines, news events, internal or external problems and windows of opportunity. Better personal organization and priority setting are crucial to success here.

I couldn't live without my smartphone and various management software programs as they help keep my first things first. I'm sure most of you would agree these crucial items help keep your daily and weekly priorities front and center.

Also anticipate the wishes of your institution's president and his or her leadership team, the deans and department chairs. Don't make them beg you to handle a specific assignment you know is on the horizon; instead, as a famous athletic sportswear brand states, just do it. This adds to your credibility.

It also demonstrates that you and your staff are on top of things – that you can face distractions and still keep lots of plates spinning at once.

Like plate-spinner Erich Brenn on "The Ed Sullivan Show," you can perform an admirable balancing act.

(An updated and expanded version of a story originally published in *CASE Currents*, March 1995. Used by permission.)

"

Asking for help isn't a sign of weakness. Instead, it's a sign of strength and plain old smarts.

"

People pay attention to influential curmudgeons. They may become your best supporters if you don't dismiss their opinion or overlook their input.

"

Become a sponge. Allow
yourself to be absorbed by your
organization's culture, traditions
and values – then respect and
honor them.

"

"

Our supporters want more from us than 'storytelling' – stories about others. They increasingly want to experience 'story living' – stories that invite them to become engaged advocates as they explore life-changing opportunities we can offer them.

Serving as the Chief Encouragement Officer

How to motivate your advancement staff

Day-to-day life in the small advancement office can be quite taxing, especially if—as is usually the case—staff members must wear many hats. Directors who want to encourage quality work, but also want to protect their staff from burnout, typically recognize the importance of implementing motivational strategies.

Motivation, by itself, will not yield success. It takes plenty of blood, sweat, and tears as well. But it *is* an essential ingredient, and as your office's leader, it's up to you to serve as the group's Chief

Encouragement Officer.

The following are five suggestions for becoming a skilled motivator:

Establish clear goals and objectives

How can you expect to motivate your staff to press forward if you don't know where you're going?

It's a lot like exploring a cave. If you enter an unfamiliar passageway with an experienced guide wielding a flashlight, your anxiety level is low. Why? Because you can see where you are going.

But as soon as that guide turns off the light to show you how *dark* dark can be, your confidence level quickly decreases. You're afraid to move forward. One step in any direction may prove to be fatal!

Goals and objectives—especially ones that reflect input from the staff—will serve as a beacon.

Lead by example

If you expect your staff to work hard and smart, you must do the same. When it's crunch time in the office, everyone—including you—should pitch in and work together to reach the common goal.

Celebrate successes – together

When your staff has met or exceeded one of its goals, celebrate *together* as a staff. Bring in a box of donuts or go out somewhere nice for lunch. We in advancement don't promote our victories enough. By conducting celebrations (and spur-of-the-moment ones are the best), you're showing your appreciation for your staff members and their tireless efforts.

When it's time to get back to the grindstone, do so. But I guarantee that your staff will return refreshed and reinvigorated because you celebrated that victory.

Empower the staff

Nothing can motivate your staff members more than when you truly empower them to do their work. Find ways to equip your employees with the knowledge and experience they need to perform their jobs successfully. Then encourage them to "step out."

I sometimes think about how my parents must have felt when they turned over the keys to our 1968 Chevrolet Impala the day I got my first driver's license. But by doing that, they demonstrated their trust in me and my decision-making abilities. I, in turn, resolved to measure up to their high expectations for me.

By empowering your staff members, you are telling them that you trust them, value their creativity and problem-solving skills, and will not become a micromanager. Empowerment can truly motivate any size advancement staff because it provides staffers with a sense of ownership in the overall program.

As the one-time head of several advancement staff offices throughout most of my professional career, I had to remind myself daily to give my staff members the freedom to make their own decisions. Was this scary for me? You bet!

But I know that those I have empowered along the way had the skills to do what was needed to be done as long because they understood the big picture – something that must continuously be communicated by you as their Chief Encouragement Officer.

Be a cheerleader

Encourage greater productivity from your already overworked, underpaid staff members by showing them constant, sincere appreciation.

In other words, roll up your sleeves and cheer your staff on to solve those daily challenges we all face. Come in the office each morning and leave in the afternoon with a smile on your face and a good word for the day.

Tell staff members how much you value their work. Thank them one on one; thank them in the presence of constituents. And always end your emails to them with "thanks."

To be your staff's Chief Communications Officer, you must be your staff's shoulder when it needs one and your staff's guide when it seeks one. Your employees will appreciate the time and interest you show in them.

(An updated and expanded version of a story originally published in *CASE Currents*, May 1999. Used by permission.)

"

Maintain a good sense of humor. It will always see you through life's ups and downs.

"

"

It's not *Desk* Relations. It's *Public* Relations. Don't allow sitting behind a computer screen keep you from meeting people face to face. Hone the skill of networking – then apply it to the profession's core mission of relationship building.

"

"

Tear down organizational silos by implementing honest, civil, constructive communication. This will build walkways and bridges of trust and collaboration.

"

Learn the skills of persuasion

and negotiation.

"

ANSWERING OPPORTUNITY'S

KNOCK

GRAB THE LOW-HANGING FRUIT FOR PUBLIC RELATIONS AND MARKETING SUCCESS

As one who enjoys reading history, I often ponder those moments of missed opportunity by myopic individuals or organizations. History is rife with such tales.

Consider the executive at Decca Records, for example, who nixed a recording contract with the legendary Beatles because he didn't see the group's musical style and compositions as unique or marketable. Or actor Nick Nolte, who reportedly turned down the role to play Indiana Jones on the big screen, allowing Harrison Ford to become the persona etched in our minds for that character.

Or when the president of the Western Union Telegraph Company passed on buying the patent to the telephone, telling Alexander Graham Bell, "We have come to the conclusion that it has no commercial possibilities."

Those of us who serve in higher education public relations and marketing must be careful not to make similar errors.

In an increasingly competitive and global higher education marketplace, it is incumbent upon those of us who manage and lead our institutional relations programs to do so with a spirit of eagerness, enthusiasm and openness, and maintain an eye for appreciating the big picture.

When opportunity knocks

It's no secret that public relations and marketing funds are tight at nearly every public and private institution across the nation. Rather than waving the proverbial white flag, we should accept this financial reality and view it as an excellent opportunity to flex our creative, professional muscle.

I have found that if I am able to demonstrate tangible results with the funds I am budgeted one fiscal year, there is a strong likelihood I will be provided a bit more funding the next year and the year after that. Success breeds success.

Forced to do more with less, we must seek out low- to no-cost public relations and marketing objectives that are high impact, efficient, effective and measurable. I have often found these to exist as low-hanging fruit staring us in the face.

When I was a child, my grandparents had a large apple tree behind their house. One year at harvest time I noticed a large, ripe apple high atop the tree, just begging for 8-year-old Marc to pick.

I conceived several crazy and, perhaps, dangerous ways to pick that apple. There was nothing wrong with me setting my sights high on that one ripe apple. Much like our professional goals, we must always aim high.

But in this case, I did not see the dozens of red, juicy apples that were right in front of my face. These apples were easily accessible from where I was standing.

If we're not careful, we may miss wonderful PR and marketing opportunities that come our way in much the same way, especially if we focus too much time and effort on the one piece of fruit high up the tree.

Perhaps actress Julie Andrews said it best: "Sometimes opportunities float right past your nose. Work hard, apply yourself and be ready. When an opportunity comes you can grab it."

Low- and no-cost strategies

Consider how you can advance your public relations and marketing program by seizing one or more of these low-hanging opportunities:

• Strategic annual planning and evaluation of communication activities, projects and initiatives;

• Cultivation of fruitful relationships with on- and off-campus constituents, including faculty, staff, media, alumni, community and governing boards;

• Productive collaborations with local and regional education, business, industry, and government for enhanced regional stewardship;

• Exemplary content that leads to effective, targeted storytelling;

• Creative, productive uses of communication technology such as various social media and video conferencing platforms.

The cost for such low-hanging fruit is practically nothing. The impact on your program and institution is priceless.

There's nothing wrong with reaching for a goal that presents itself as a challenge. After all, we grow by stretching ourselves. Our first challenge, though, should be to seize as many low-hanging opportunities as possible before proceeding to the high, lofty ones.

I guarantee you and your president will celebrate marked improvements with your school's total institutional relations program as you harvest the low-hanging fruit.

———————————————————————————

(An updated and expanded version of a story originally published in *University Business*. Used by permission.)

"

Expect moments of failure and
learn from them.

"

"

From time-to-time, we all take shrapnel during our career. Become battled tested, not battle-worn.

"

Write, write and write. The more you write, the better skilled you will become.

"

"

Always be honest. Anything less than 100 percent is unacceptable.

KEEPING PR-FIT THROUGHOUT THE ACADEMIC YEAR

TEACH A COURSE AND OTHER TIPS FOR LEARNING AND BECOMING BETTER AT YOUR JOB

For the first few months of a New Year, many of us are eager to get physically fit. And those of us who work in PR and marketing must stay professionally fit by remaining relevant to meet and even surpass those needs our institutions will always have. We must stay ahead of the curve as we present ourselves as strategic communicator whose expertise and counsel can be trusted.

Here are a few important ways you, as a public relations or marketing professional, can remain professionally fit for this year and for the future:

Read, and read some more

Learning is truly a lifelong process. Keep fresh in your work by reading current books, articles, white papers, blogs, and various social media postings. This not only will keep your mind active and stir creative juices, but will educate you on the latest trends in the profession. Per Dr. Seuss' admonishment: "The more that you read, the more things you will know. The more that you learn, the more places you'll go."

Teach a course

If you can do it, teaching a course in communications is another terrific way to remain fit. The benefits of doing so far outweigh the time it takes for class preparation. Teaching a course during the semester or summer months allows you to know your No. 1 customer—students—more intimately. As they share their view of the world, you will no doubt learn more from them than they learn from you.

In addition, you will become an even more respected and trusted colleague with members of the faculty as you listen to their goals, aspirations, ideas, academic achievements and challenges. Lastly, teaching will encourage you to remain fresh in the literature as you study and prepare for class time.

Go outside your world

Jack Welch, retired chairman and CEO of General Electric, said: "An organization's ability to learn, and translate that learning into action rapidly, is the ultimate competitive advantage." Taking time to visit successful corporations, industries, small businesses, nonprofit organizations, and colleges and universities of all types can sharpen your creative edge. All of us can learn from others' successes. Consider ways you can modify their successes for your own program's application.

Become tech savvy

Millennials are quite comfortable with

technology, and it is vital that baby boomer professionals become just as comfortable and familiar with its applications. We must not fall prey to saying, "I don't do social media."

Enroll in professional development workshops

Jump into the technology swimming pool—and learn by trial and error. A significant part of a public relations and marketing professional's work is now conducted through various digital communication technologies. The more we learn and apply those technologies to our everyday work, the more effective and efficient we will become.

Write often

Writing has always been at the heart of our work. Because public relations and marketing professionals in higher education are expected to create and develop content that is compelling, accurate and timely, it is important that we continually stretch our writing muscles. Whether it's an op-ed for a local newspaper, a blog post or a speech you draft, take time each day to write.

Get out of the office

Last, but certainly not least, do not take up professional residence behind your desk. Our work, after all, is "public" relations, not "desk" relations. Despite the advances and conveniences of technology, our work is centered around establishing and maintaining relationships for our institutions. We can easily be lulled into the notion that our work is done as long as we can communicate with others via email, texts, video calling or social media.

Make sure to dedicate time each day to meet one-on-one with your institution's various constituents.

They will better value what you do and, in return, you will gain a greater appreciation for them as you share your institution's success story to an eager audience.

(An updated and expanded version of a story originally published in *University Business*. Used by permission.)

"

Read as much as you can. The quality and depth of your conversations will deepen and become more meaningful as you broaden your understanding of the world around you.

"

Become skilled at managing crises. It's one of the best ways to sharpen your skills as a public relations professional.

"

"

Don't throw the baby out with the bathwater. Seek a balanced approach to your communication efforts by blending traditional and digital means.

"

"

Our world is starved for
principle-centered, servant
leadership. Become that leader.

"

THE RELATIONSHIP-BUILDING

BUSINESS

PR PROFESSIONALS HAVE AN ARRAY OF TOOLS—BOTH OLD AND NEW—AT THEIR DISPOSAL

Facebook is knocking on the door of turning 20 as the social networking service was launched on February 4, 2004.

I remember how thrilled I was when 25 people had requested to be my friend by the end of my first day on Facebook. Since that time, I have become heavily engaged in social networking, and have established and maintained relationships through platforms such as Twitter, LinkedIn, Instagram, Tumblr and, of course, Facebook. They are incredible tools for communication.

I will be the first to admit that communicating via text, email and social media is a great help in pushing information far beyond what we could in those not-so-long-ago days before the web. However, we can ill afford to allow those methods to become the only way we connect with people. Instead, they should be included in the collection of tools we use to build interactive relationships.

Multiple approaches

For those of us in the public relations and marketing professions, we must constantly remind ourselves we are in the relationship-building business. As humans, our DNA makeup craves face-to-face interaction.

Today's young adults are the most "connected" generation in the history of our planet, and yet they have been tagged the "lonely generation." Why? The reason is simple: We crave interaction like our bodies crave water and food.

Relationships nourish us and make us complete,

but they suffer without face-to-face interaction. When that's not possible, however, we turn to the next best thing that encourages productive communication and gains effective, measurable results.

How then can we stay true to our role as relationship builders while driving on this digital communication expressway? Here are a few tips for blending the online and face-to-face worlds. Use these strategies in your interactions with administrators, faculty and students, as well as the media and broader community.

Lunch or coffee meeting

Some would argue that having a meeting over a meal or coffee is nothing more than a waste of time and money. I disagree. Such encounters are great for establishing, building or renewing meaningful business relationships for any organization, including colleges and universities. Nothing can break down barriers better than a shared meal or a cup of hot joe.

Handwritten note

What's old is new. A well-written note placed in the mail is a wonderful way to convey warmth and personalization. A handwritten note can have more impact than shooting off a quick email expressing your appreciation for exceptional service or a job well done.

Videoconferencing

This technology really is "the next best thing to being there." Videoconferencing offers great communication opportunities that were previously unavailable.

Zoom, FaceTime, Skype and other platforms can bring you face-to-face with constituents anywhere. All you need is a computer, a webcam and a place to talk. Seeing and hearing one another promotes mutual understanding and credibility.

Once this relationship has been established, you can use other tools in your communication mix to continue the relationship.

Social networking

I don't mean "one-way and you're done" communication. That's typically how social media works. Social networking, however, is all about engaging and nourishing the relationship.

To incorporate social networking into your institutions' PR and marketing operations, it should be viewed as a strategic communication process.

For example, I am a huge fan of LinkedIn. Rather than "collecting people" as some do when requesting a connection, I see it as a platform that can build relationships effectively. If someone follows me on Twitter, I will automatically seek to establish a connection with them via LinkedIn.

If I've met someone while attending a workshop or conference, or have exchanged a few emails or phone calls with a new contact, I will immediately request a LinkedIn connection before they forget who I am.

From there, I try to strategically conceive of PR

and marketing opportunities that might engage my new connection into the life of my institution. Once I have established a connection with someone on LinkedIn, I typically will contact them via Skype or invite them to the campus for a one-on-one meeting so that our business relationship can mature.

(An updated and expanded version of a story originally published in *University Business*. Used by permission.)

"

People expect excellent service.
Be exceptional and you'll be
remembered… and invited
back.

"

"

Keep yourself fresh and relevant in the communication profession. Learning doesn't stop with the college diploma.

"

"

Lead by example. Integrity and character come first. After all, your name is all you really own and control.

"

"

Be actively engaged in the life of your community and organization. The investment of your time will reap from colleagues their faith, trust and confidence in you.

"

Building a campus' proactive crisis communications program

How a solid crisis plan can advance the PR office's reputation and credibility

It had begun like most fall mornings on a college campus. The air was crisp and the sky was clear as students, faculty and staff prepared for another day. The difference this day was that a host of state and local police officers, EMTs and paramedics had converged on the administration building. A staff member had been found dead, an apparent suicide, just an hour before classes began.

News of the incident quickly spread across the small campus and moved throughout the community. Chatter on social media sparked rumors of a gunman atop the administration building, firing down at students. The college's switchboard came alive with calls from frantic parents and various media outlets.

Within 30 minutes, however, the college's public relations office, working with law enforcement, the coroner and president's office, had provided the community with details of the tragic incident that had taken place. Like turning water off at a faucet, rumors and fears had been allayed. A state police officer later described it as "textbook crisis communications management at its best."

Just three weeks earlier, the college's first crisis communications plan had been presented to the cabinet. For those of us who serve as spokespersons for our institutions, it is important that we have communication procedures in place to manage a campus crisis.

Proactive approach

Crisis communications management is often a reactive measure. But the most effective public relations managers are those who are proactive. These tips can help as you develop a proactive crisis communications plan:

Talk to your president

Understand the president's expectation of your role and how you should communicate when there are warning signs of a possible crisis—or when one actually occurs.

Meet often with campus leaders

It is important that key players, including vice presidents, deans and department chairs, know who you are and how you manage your public relations operation.

Develop strong relations with the media

Reporters must know they can count on you to provide honest, accurate and timely information in a crisis.

Maintain good relations with key safety personnel

Meet often with your institution's public safety and risk management officers, as well as with your local community's chiefs of police and fire operations. Long before any incident occurs, they need to know who you are and how you manage crisis communications.

Be aware of potential situations

This can be achieved by monitoring social media and listening to students, faculty and staff. Analyze the information and determine whether it warrants reporting to the president and members of the cabinet. Often a communication crisis can be prevented if there is time to respond internally.

Don't give more life to a crisis than it deserves

It is far better that you confront it in a timely way and note how your institution plans to address the matter. When proactively managed, your crisis will be significantly reduced.

Hone your personal skills

Do you present yourself as a steady, calm, articulate, mature voice for your institution? What might you do better the next time? Take note of how corporations and other colleges and universities handle crises.

Review your plan

It should include contact information for key constituents, the crisis communications team, emergency personnel, local officials, media contacts and campus leadership. It should note web and social media accounts managed by your institution's public relations and public safety offices. Keep the plan updated to reflect changes in personnel on- and off-campus.

Do a follow-up

After a crisis, take time to ask those involved— including the media, law enforcement and emergency agencies—to critique your institution's communications efforts. This will help to better position the institution and the public relations office as trustworthy organizations during smooth and not-so-smooth times.

(An updated and expanded version of a story originally published in *University Business*. Used by permission.)

"

Seek a mentor. Become a
mentor.

"

Planning is not an option. It's essential. Working without a plan is like walking into a cave and failing to bring a flashlight.

"

"

All good communication plans may have your initial touch. But exceptional plans include many fingerprints.

"

"

If you come with a problem, be ready to offer the solution.

"

In Crisis Communications Management, It's the Small Things that Matter

L egendary UCLA basketball coach John Wooden said, "It's the little details that are vital. Little things make big things happen."

Such may be said of seeing to the finer details of crisis communications management. We all agree that advance planning can head off unwanted administrative headaches and chaotic public relations responses when we face those unforeseen campus crises that can interrupt a perfectly tranquil day.

Incorporating a few select aspects to your institution's overall crisis communications plan will allow your public relations office to be more proactive on the day when emergency and communications management responses are required. Seeing to small details should not be viewed as an added, unnecessary effort. Rather, they should be seen as strategies that will lead to protecting the institution's reputation and image.

Consider implementing these five details in your college or university's overall crisis communications plan for complete, well-executed success.

Test your host community's emergency systems and protocols

Never assume your local community's emergency response systems and protocols will automatically complement your institution's crisis response plan. It is advisable that your crisis response team meet on a quarterly basis with local officials to review crisis communications procedures. Such meetings can uncover aspects of planning that are essential: How much stress can local landlines and cellular phone towers take from sudden, massive calls? What are agreed upon emergency road routes that lead away from the campus and community? How soon can utility services be restored to campus facilities should electric and water services be interrupted? Who becomes the spokesperson should the host community become involved in your campus crisis?

Personally know the agency heads of local and state emergency responders

The last thing you want or have time for as the institutional spokesperson is to arrive on the scene of a campus emergency and the city police or fire chief, utilities director or state police officer asks, "Who are you?" As the college or university's chief public relations officer, you cannot afford to be an unknown or vaguely familiar figure. In times of emergency, you must be a known and respected authority whom officials recognize as soon as you arrive. Frequent and consistent meetings with the chiefs of local and state emergency responders will quickly advance the respect and trust you must have as your institution's spokesperson. A crisis situation is no time to introduce yourself.

Media training for administrative officers and academic deans is critical

Take time to provide media training for all members of your institution's administrative and academic leadership. Waiting to coach them when a campus crisis occurs is not the time and could result in ill-advised and potentially reputation-damaging comments. Proper media relations training will enable your institution to respond to news reporters in a professional, timely and proactive manner. Consider asking your public relations office to coordinate such an ongoing exercise. Such training can be provided by the institution's professional PR staff or by an outside agency that specializes in media skill development.

Pre- and post-crisis communications reviews with local media

It is important for your institution and its public relations operation to gain trust and respect from media organizations in your area and state. This trust and respect can be gained in various ways. But as the institution's chief public relations officer seeks to address crisis communications details, regular meetings with media organizations is a wise investment in one's professional time. Take time during the "quiet days" to learn how your local and state media organizations prefer working with your institution's PR office during a crisis situation. I have always found media meetings a week or so following such a situation is also helpful to see where communication services might be improved. You are not required to accept everything that is shared with you. Such meetings, however, encourage dialogue between the institution and the media, and generally result in greater respect and appreciation for one another.

Plan the work and work the plan

An annual review and updating of an institution's crisis communications plan is strongly advisable. Contact information for names of administrative and academic heads may change. New crisis scenarios may arise. And advanced emergency technologies and social media channels may need to be integrated into your existing plan. All plans can benefit from a good spring cleaning!

Never underestimate how powerfully important seeing to the details can be in crisis communications. With advance preparation, you can prevent bad situations from becoming even worse.

"

Go out of your way each day to help, encourage, love or celebrate someone. Kindness never falls out of fashion.

"

"

Whenever one thinks they have arrived, they have – at the foot of disaster. Take your work seriously, but not yourself. Celebrate your successes, but don't get too overconfident.

"

"

No one is a self-made person. We're where we are because someone along the way sacrificed or helped open a door of opportunity for us.

"

"

Details matter.

"

Strategies to Build Town-Gown Relations

As long-time neighbors, we simply take one another for granted

I n our efforts to market and communicate with our various constituents, we often overlook one of the most important support groups we have—our college town.

It's not intentional. As long-time neighbors, we simply take one another for granted. But that's changing as institutions and their local governments look to one another for creative ways to collaborate and maximize financial and capital resources.

Colleges and universities are typically the

economic engines that drive the quality of life in their local towns. They tend to attract a diverse population, ranging from young professionals to retired senior adults. They also encourage industrial research and development, a better mix of retail and vast opportunities in the arts and athletics.

The need and desire for universities and their communities to become better dance partners has led to the creation of a nonprofit association focused solely on establishing and enhancing better community relations—the International Town and Gown Association, based in Clemson, South Carolina.

The ITGA's network of resources is helping more than 200 colleges, universities and municipal governments come together on issues such as mixed-use development opportunities, the quality of life around the edge of campus and in off-campus housing areas, and sharing water, fire, police and other services.

"We are seeing town-gown relations being strengthened in communities around areas that are of common interest and benefit," says ITGA Executive Director Beth Bagwell. "College towns are growing economically through stronger university-community partnerships that nurture startups and promote regional/local economic development opportunities."

Successful town-gown efforts do not happen overnight. They take time, commitment, patience, creativity and a willingness from both parties to give and take. College and university public relations and marketing professionals can play an instrumental role in developing and enhancing these relations:

Establish a "Town-Gown Commission" consisting of representatives from the community, university and municipality to share ideas and address common challenges. This body will carry more weight if the local mayor and the college's president jointly give it their charge and appoint the executive team.

Become a strategic communicator for both your president and mayor by keeping them abreast of current or emerging issues on and off campus.

Schedule forums involving the mayor and president. Invite the mayor to conduct a forum on campus that involves the student government association. Likewise, the president should consider holding a forum off campus with the local chamber of commerce or city council.

Invite university and civic leaders to quarterly community leadership breakfasts. Breaking bread while discussing town-gown issues can resolve issues more quickly and be an excellent way to energize these leaders as they become better acquainted.

Become actively involved with one or more community organizations. As your institution's spokesperson, your involvement demonstrates the institution's sincere interest in improving quality of life in your college town.

Strategically prepare and place news stories that highlight town-gown collaborations. Community media and student newspapers are often eager to publish such and they often make for excellent social media posts that can carry far beyond your city limits. This can help you brand your college town as being among the nation's best.

When engaging your institution with the host community, be smart and targeted, use your time effectively and efficiently, and make things happen for your institution's leadership.

Keep the local media well informed and involved in the life of your institution. That includes being transparent about the occasional not-so-good news moments, too, as this helps build mutual trust.

As your institution's public relations and marketing professional, be a cheer leader for your community and university. You can position your president, institutional leadership and yourself as the complete town-gown ambassadors. Your institution and host community will both benefit from the relationship.

(An updated and expanded version of a story originally published in *University Business*. Used by permission.)

"

Sitting at the Big Table demands one to be a critical, creative thinker and strategic communicator, not merely a tactical manager.

"

"

Don't fear trying new ideas,
exploring new directions or
making new friends.

"

"

In social media, don't be a 'follower collector.' Be a 'people engager.'

"

"

Learn to hold confidences well. Once you do, you'll become a trusted, valued member of the team.

TOURISM: A COLLEGE MARKETING GOLDMINE

CAPITALIZE ON TOWN-GOWN RELATIONS FOR HIGHER EDUCATION PR AND MARKETING SUCCESS

College towns across the country may be sitting on an economic and tourism marketing gold mine in the form of their local institution's "tourist attractions."

Consider the thousands of people who go to a school's concerts, theatrical performances, athletic events, museums, planetarium shows, camps and conferences—not to mention those visiting for homecoming, family weekends and daily admissions visits.

A steady flow of college town "tourists" directly benefits the local economy with dollars spent on dining, shopping, entertainment and hotels.

Tourism is big business. According to the U.S. Travel Association, direct spending on leisure travel by domestic and international travelers totaled $761.7 billion in 2018. Spending on leisure travel generated $117.4 billion in tax revenue.

In cities and towns that host one of the nation's 4,000-plus public and private institutions, civic and university officials should try to capture a share of this bustling tourism market.

Collaboration

How might your institution and the community's tourism office capitalize on your college to drive tourism? Consider these ideas:

• First and foremost, realize you need one another. Regular dialogue is essential and is the most important planning component when determining joint aspirations.

- Formalize a relationship between your institution and the tourism office. Your public relations and marketing offices can provide campus brochures, maps, event schedules and photos for display.

- Explore other college towns for creative ideas that might be relevant to your community.

- Become involved in the planning and preparation process for university-sponsored events that will impact the community's restaurant, retail, transportation and lodging industries, along with nearby tourist attractions.

- Create a kiosk in the tourism office featuring institutional memorabilia and information. Visitors often look to the tourism office for information regarding the local college or university. It is best to be prepared when you roll out the welcome mat.

- Develop and conduct a historic community tour that includes your campus. This is a great way to bridge town-gown relations, and perhaps involve college retirees interested in volunteering their time and love of their institution.

- Work with the tourism office to establish student internships for public relations, communications and hospitality majors.

- Seek co-branding opportunities that promote both the tourism office and the college. Streetlight banners are a terrific way to brand yourself as a college town.

- Engage local restaurants and lodging facilities. They can become some of your best and most effective town-gown advocates if they know what is happening on campus and in town.

- Familiarize civic and campus leaders with the community. Never assume they know key points of campus and community interest.

- Invite outsiders to evaluate your tourism efforts. A "secret shopper" could provide your tourism office with critical information.

- Develop print and electronic versions of your community's visitors guide, and include important campus information.

- The tourism office and university public relations should conduct an annual review of your strategy. Prune what's not working, and develop ideas that will generate interest in the town and campus.

Community foundation

In his 2014 book, *Town & Gown: From Conflict to Cooperation*, author Michael Fox wrote: "Quality of life and economic prosperity are the foundation of strong communities, and places that are home to universities and colleges have a significant edge on attracting."

This attraction can significantly influence a college town's ability to recruit business and research. With cooperation, dialogue, planning and execution, your college town's tourism program will help make your institution—and its host town—a desired destination.

(An updated and expanded version of a story originally published in *University Business*. Used by permission.)

"

In social media, don't fret about those who don't or won't follow you. Instead, be engaged with those who do. You will reap the results.

"

"

Catch someone doing something good today. Let them know their efforts are making a difference in others' lives, the organization or both.

"

Think in terms of movements, not campaigns. Campaigns are limited by time and rely on traditional methods. Movements are fed by passion and rely on word of mouth.

"

"

No matter how large or small your institution or organization might be, a good story is a good story. Pitch boldly!

"

HARNESSING THE POWER OF SOCIAL MEDIA

TIPS FOR POWER USERS AND NEWBIES ON RUNNING A SUCCESSFUL SOCIAL NETWORKING PROGRAM

Without a doubt, social media has become one of the, if not the most, effective and efficient way for colleges and universities to communicate. Connected institutions can conduct "digital conversations" while sharing and collecting thoughts, ideas, information, opinions, images and video.

The implications for higher education marketing, public relations, admissions, alumni outreach and development operations are staggering. By strategically developing and enhancing relationships with your constituents with the help of a robust social media program, colleges and universities can garner interest and support never before imagined from all reaches of the globe.

Get the most from social media

Whether your institution is actively engaged in social networking or just starting out, these tips should help you achieve optimum return on your investment:

Define your purpose

First and foremost, social media is about relationship-building and engagement. Commit to using your digital network as an opportunity to engage constituents in the life of your institution.

Go slowly

Do not launch multiple social media platforms at once. Add a second one only if the first is established and successful—then grow your social media platforms from there. It is far better to launch and manage one or two social media accounts well rather than do three or more poorly. Do not fall prey to launching several social media platforms simply because a competitor has done so.

Eliminate "fluff" posts

Make sure your content is interesting and relevant for your audience and worthy to be shared with wider social network users. Spread "awesome," not "meh."

Establish a social media "personality"

Ever known someone who acts a certain way one day and is the complete opposite the next, only to revert to the initial personality the following day? It can be confusing and frustrating. The same holds true when developing a personality for your social media. Be consistent with the tone and look of your content, as well as with any images or videos you post.

Promote your expertise

Target traditional and digital media outlets and

respected bloggers, and demonstrate your institution's public relations office as a credible news source for them by the content you post. Your role as the institution's primary storyteller cannot be underestimated.

Keep content fresh and relevant

Similar to maintaining fresh content on your website, your social media deserves attention every day. Your friends, followers and the social network peers expect it. Therefore, frequently and consistently post content when your constituents will most likely read and share your postings.

Be extremely cautious about deleting negative comments

We all seek positive feedback. A negative comment posted on social media can often cause fear and panic, and lead some to immediately call for its removal. In today's digital world, that negative comment can just as easily be posted elsewhere. I call this the "haunting effect," as a quick deletion can come back to haunt us elsewhere on the internet. Institutions hold varying opinions about handling negative comments on social media. Whatever position you might hold, always remember that the haunting effect can be greatly reduced if a timely, reasonable and mature institutional response is given to the critic.

Measure and evaluate the effectiveness of your social media platforms

Quantitative and qualitative data provide valuable information as you monitor your social media progress.

Don't pull the plug on traditional media

Television, newspapers and radio continue to attract significant audiences. A balanced approach is a smarter way to go as you engage millennials, Gen Xers and baby boomers.

Have fun and communicate

Don't view social media as a chore. It is about connecting and having a genuine conversation with those who are interested in your institution. Strike up a conversation and be responsive to your friends and followers.

(An updated and expanded version of a story originally published in *University*

Business. Used by permission.)

"

Mutual trust, respect, transparency, timeliness and accuracy are essential ingredients for healthy relations.

"

"

Occasionally, go outside your world to better expand your knowledge and expertise.

"

"

Grab the low-hanging fruit
before seeking the apple at the
top of the tree. Great PR and
marketing opportunities are
often dangling in front of us.
Don't overlook them.

"

"

Find some me-time. There's
only one you. Take care of
yourself and those relationships
that mean so much to you.

"

IT'S NOT ALL DIGITAL IN COLLEGE BRANDING

VALUING THE ROLE OF CAMPUS GROUNDS, TOURS AND PHONE ETIQUETTE IN THE DIGITAL MARKETING AGE

Few of us could imagine where we would be in our institutional branding efforts without the internet and its related marketing and public relations applications. These digital tools have become our "digital front doors," granting us the ability to effectively and efficiently share content with those eager to learn more about us.

With that said, I also offer a word of caution: We cannot fail to recognize, respect and groom three non-digital yet vital areas of institutional branding, all of which have significant value.

Maintaining grounds and facilities

Campus appearance is crucial to an institution's branding identity. Not only do well-landscaped, handsomely manicured grounds and well-maintained facilities create a positive work environment, they attract and retain students, faculty, staff and donors.

First impressions are critical. Studies have long confirmed that the appearance of an institution's grounds and facilities are among the most influential factors when families are determining whether to invest time and resources.

Attractive entranceways, consistent signage, maintenance of landscaped areas and sidewalks, and well-kept facilities—inside and out—speak volumes to visitors about the quality, sense of care and level of stewardship we seek to present. They communicate that we are worth a student's or donor's investment.

The campus tour

Most admissions counselors agree that if you can bring a student to campus for a visit, your chances of successfully recruiting them have significantly increased. Once a student commits to a visit, make sure you can deliver on your end.

Recruit enthusiastic, positive, knowledgeable and articulate counselors or students as your tour guides. As your campus "sales force," they must be well-trained professionals who clearly understand their role.

If tour guides are asked questions they can't answer, it is perfectly fine to admit that. Being honest and forthright is always the best policy. Do promise an answer and respond in a timely manner—prospective students and parents appreciate honesty and integrity, and can typically spot whenever neither is demonstrated.

Better customer service

Perhaps one of the most overlooked areas of institutional branding is phone management.

Good or bad, we leave a lasting impression on those who call us for information or assistance.

There is a direct correlation between our branding reputation and the level of professionalism, responsiveness and tone we use when assisting people who call us.

I experienced this several years ago while preparing an article for a national news agency. The story required the expertise of a professor at a well-respected, nationally branded institution.

My mental image of this institution reflected nothing less than academe at its finest. But when I called, a person answered the office phone by saying: "Yep."

At first, I thought I'd misdialed. So I apologized and explained I had called the wrong number. After making sure I punched the correct numbers, the same person answered, only to ask: "Yep. Whaddaya want?"

After listening to a series of grunted replies, I was eventually transferred to the professor for the interview. I must admit, though, my impression of that institution was tarnished simply because of the poor way the phone was answered. (In fairness, I suspect most of its other offices answered their phones correctly.)

Here's what we should remember:

- Never underestimate the power of the simple phone call.

- Don't allow the voice messaging system to become the only voice the caller receives. A live voice adds a touch of personal attention.

- Ongoing training/etiquette are essential.

When we fully integrate digital media's public relations and marketing tools with exceptional grounds and facilities, admissions visits, and phone etiquette, we will then realize the branding reputation that truly distinguishes us in a highly competitive marketplace.

(An updated and expanded version of a story originally published in *University Business*. Used by permission.)

"

Keep calm and communicate on! Those around you will respond and mirror your behavior during times of crisis and challenge.

"

Flexibility keeps you from breaking.

"

"

Always remember to say 'thank you.' Be grateful. It's the right thing to do. Besides, your mom will be proud of you!

"

"

When communicating with the public, don't use jargons and acronyms. Your audience may or may not understand them. Speak or write the language of the people. That's communication.

"

Higher education partnerships promise fundraising success

Philanthropy and communications teams must work together to promote the mission

Most of us would agree that much can be achieved when we work together. In the case of philanthropy and communications staff, we both desire that our constituencies become enthusiastic supporters and advocates of our institution. It is imperative that these professionals become partners in every sense. Here's how.

Step 1: Philanthropy and communications staff must understand and appreciate each

other's roles

I recall a story from 20 years ago in which a vice president for advancement at a private college was concerned that his philanthropy officers and his communications team were sailing on the same lake, but in different boats. To set a different, more productive course, he called the advancement staff together for a joint Friday meeting.

Beginning the following Monday, he said, the communications staff would shadow philanthropy for two weeks. Then the philanthropy staff would shadow their communications comrades the following two weeks.

This vice president wanted his communications officers to become more knowledgeable about the art, science and challenges of fundraising, and vice versa. And from all reports, the experiment was successful.

In the speed and demands of today's higher education landscape, few institutions can afford to grant the time such an experiment requires.

However, the lesson learned remains relevant.

Various surveys indicate that communications and philanthropy teams at colleges, universities and other nonprofits perform their given tasks well, but often lack expertise or understanding of the other's craft. By sitting down together on a frequent and consistent basis, they will achieve greater trust and a deeper understanding of what can be achieved—together.

Step 2: Develop a philanthropy communications plan

When building this plan, involve those who fundraise for your institution as well as those who oversee the communications and marketing functions. Make sure to consider your donors and prospects, and what messaging and communication tools work best for them.

When it's time to evaluate your plan, measure its success as a joint philanthropy/communications team, not as two or three siloed groups. This approach will encourage the team to better appreciate each other's "language"—resulting in the creation of a common voice that donors will understand and value.

Step 3: Consider the brand

With the first two steps underway, you must always be cognizant of how your efforts will convey the institution's brand to alumni, friends and parents, among others. The stories, words, phrases, themes and images incorporated in your philanthropy communication efforts must support, not distract from, the overarching identity and messaging of your institution.

In the 2002 movie *Drumline*, fictional Atlanta A&T University band director James Lee repeatedly reminded his students that to produce magnificent music, they had to play as "one band, one sound." Our constituencies, too, depend on us performing as "one band" with "one sound."

Once these three steps become standard procedure, you will begin seeing exciting and measurable results that benefit the institution's brand and its fundraising efforts. It has been said: "When you discover your mission, you will feel its demand. It will fill you with enthusiasm and a burning desire to get to work on it."

This, too, may be said of our donors. When they discover our institution's mission and sense its aspirations—coupled with their enthusiasm and burning desire to make a marked difference—they, along with your institution, will succeed.

(An updated and expanded version of a story originally published in *University Business*. Used by permission.)

"

Our work makes a difference in
the life of our organization and
the lives of others.

"

"

You don't always have to have the best ideas or answers in the room. But you should always be ready to offer such or spark dialogue.

"

"

Our world has been waiting for
your contribution. Seize this
moment.

"

"

Be an idea planter and
cultivator.

"

A COMMUNICATIONS PLAN AND COLLABORATIONS CAN HELP NAVIGATE AND SUPPORT LONG-LASTING DONOR RELATIONSHIPS

Philanthropy represents the best of humankind. It promotes the welfare of others while encouraging people to give generously and selflessly to worthy organizations such as yours.

In all of your philanthropy or donor-focused communications, you must seek to create a connection between your organization and the donor or prospect around shared values. You should inform, demonstrate the impact of the donor's investment, foster donor trust and advance a culture of philanthropy within your institution or nonprofit.

Communication that is compelling plays a critical role in igniting philanthropists' interest and desire to support our institution or organization. It helps to not only attract donors but retain and increase their involvement and partnership.

Effective, productive philanthropy or donor communication:

• Issues a clear call to action for funding and volunteer support

• Promotes a unified message and visual identity

• Sparks interest among donors and other constituents

• Stimulates school pride (if you're a college or university)

• Builds and strengthens relationships while creating a robust, sustainable base of supporters

• Rallies people to support the cause and campaign or movement

- Shares how philanthropy is making a difference (e.g., storytelling, testimonials, etc.)

- Recognizes philanthropy support and advances donor relations and stewardship efforts

In recognition of this, an effective philanthropy communications plan can support the university or nonprofit organization by:

- Advancing the mission

- Establishing and maintaining organizational credibility

- Strategically planning communication goals and objectives that benefit internal parties and external constituencies

- Reinforcing donor confidence by maintaining organizational transparency

- Informing and raising awareness about the institution or organization's priorities and opportunities.

To accomplish this goal of intentional, effective and targeted philanthropy messaging, you should enlist the help of your university's colleges and units, working individually and collectively with the communications and philanthropy officers to create central themes that shine through all philanthropy print and digital content.

As mentioned in the previous chapter, all of this can be achieved whenever communications and philanthropy (public relations and development) officers work hand-in-hand. It's through that partnership that philanthropy communications can and *will* soar.

When these two partners work together to execute successful philanthropy communications efforts—including capital campaign and specially-designated days such as #GivingTuesday—your institution or organization will be better prepared to:

- Identify and produce crucial philanthropy messaging;

- Coordinate and post effective and consistent social media content; and

- Manage productive media relations initiatives.

This will then result in all communication arms of an organization better prepared to consistently use unified messaging and themes while promoting the same goals and maximizing the effectiveness and creating a sustaining a culture of philanthropy at your workplace.

A well-organized and well-executed philanthropy or donor communications plan further enhances a positive culture and climate for giving. It provides a targeted approach, sending the right messages to the right audiences, conveying the right objectives at the right times.

College and department collaborations with PR and philanthropy offices

No doubt your public relations operation is always seeking ways to collaborate with its colleges and departments, or if you're a nonprofit, the staff units.

I'm sure you've already found what can be

achieved through collaborations within your organization. Here are but a few ways internal partnerships can have a positive impact on your philanthropy communications:

- Posting of unified content on social media channels

- Sharing of fundraising news, updates, information, photos, videos and feature stories and organizational print and digital publications

- Repurposing of content

- Marketing of podcasts

- Instituting old-fashioned, yet effective, speakers bureaus.

Philanthropy communications story, web content, social media, photos and editorial filters

To maintain consistency and achieve intended results, consider applying one or more of the following "editorial filters" when preparing stories, blogs, podcasts, web content, social media, photos or videos. Please ask yourself:

1. How does it impact your organization's strategic plan?

2. How does it support the goals and objectives of your capital campaign, annual giving or estate planning efforts?

3. Is this a presidential or senior-level priority for the institution?

4. What measure of significance has philanthropy played?

5. Is this the result of a donor's dream?

6. Will students, faculty, staff, researchers, alumni, parents or communities (including your local community) benefit from the philanthropy?

7. Is the content prepared from the donor's perspective or the organization's?

8. How can we make the content appear more personalized?

9. Is the content conversational in tone and easy-to-follow?

"

Measure, evaluate and continually communicate your progress with the team. Don't overlook the lasting value of internal communication with your staff and senior leadership.

"

Don't dismiss the importance of first impressions. Always come prepared.

"

"

Anticipate. Plan ahead. Understand the dynamics of the room. Be observant at all times.

"

"

Micromanagement is the best way to tell your staff: 'I don't trust you.' Hire the best. Share the big picture. Then step back and allow them to soar. You, your team and organization will greatly benefit from your faith and trust in them.

"

'ONE SIZE FITS ALL' NO LONGER APPLIES FOR EFFECTIVE HIGHER EDUCATION DONOR COMMUNICATIONS

GENERATIONAL DIFFERENCES SHOULD GUIDE TODAY'S PHILANTHROPY MARKETING EFFORTS

Have you noticed a recent change in fashion? I'm talking about a subtle yet important change with ball caps. That's right—ball caps.

In the market for one recently, I scoured a sporting goods store's display of ball caps, and discovered one small, but significant, difference. For many years, ball caps came with the tag sewn inside the inner rim: "one size fits all."

So, regardless if you had a small head or a large one like mine, you could take a chance purchasing a ball cap that would hopefully fit—even if that meant the adjustable strap was stretched to its last hole. Being sensitive to changes in the marketplace, sporting goods manufacturers now produce ball caps with the tag: "one size fits most."

That's an important difference as ball cap designers have recognized that people and their interests and needs are not all the same— particularly the shape and size of their heads.

This same lesson is a relevant one, too, for higher education philanthropy, as well as for alumni and parental marketing and communications efforts, thanks to the seismic sociological changes that a multigenerational America is now experiencing.

Changing times

For more than 80 years, our nation has been guided by the values, needs, interests and cultural backgrounds of the generations known as baby boomers (born between 1946 and 1964) and the silent generation (born before 1946). Until the emergence of GenX and millennials, silents and boomers dictated much of the marketplace's consumer demands.

In response, colleges and universities developed academic programs, student services, messaging, special events and facilities that appealed to this massive generation that was spawned by a post-World War II baby boom. But times have changed and so must the ways we communicate with multigenerational donors.

We must be ever mindful of messages and themes that best resonate with baby boomers and millennials, and strategically communicate and market to them accordingly.

In a 2018 Pew Research Center white paper, "How Millennials today compare with their grandparents 50 years ago," authors Richard Fry, Ruth Igielnik and Eileen Patten noted that this new generation of adults has become "more detached from major institutions such as political parties, religion, the military and marriage. At the same time, the racial and ethnic makeup of the country has changed, college attainment has spiked and women have greatly increased their participation in the nation's workforce."

Among a few of the generational differences noted by Fry, Igielnik and Patten were:

• A greater share of millennial women have a bachelor's degree than their male counterparts and are much more likely to be working (a reversal from the silent generation)

• A greater share of millennials today live in metropolitan areas than did silents and baby boomers when they were young adults.

Targeting a diverse population

In light of these demographic changes, we must take a hard look at how we strategically communicate with our donors, alumni and parents, while targeting their generational interests and values. No longer can we adhere to a "one size fits all" communication strategy if we expect to engage our multigenerational supporters.

Remember to always market to your audience. This by no means is a new, revolutionary idea. When you apply the right ingredients to your donor communications, you will always turn out an effort that not only is attractive, but connects with the tastes and appetite of your supporters.

(An updated and expanded version of a story originally published in *University Business*. Used by permission.)

"

In planning communication strategies, it's vital we always seek ways to build relationships.

"

"

In our profession, continually think about the 'next step, the next opportunity.'

"

"

Start strong. Finish stronger.

"

Colleges get to know their audience

Personalized marketing strategies grab the attention of donors and alumni

No doubt you have received a wall or desk calendar from your alma mater. Such calendars often feature campus scenes that trigger memories of student days.

Recently, my wife, a second-grade teacher, received a desk calendar unlike any I had seen before, from a nonprofit education group she supports. What caught my attention was that the calendar's front cover featured my wife's first name; so did each month. Every page featured a photograph with an object designed around her name.

One month had wooden building blocks stacked and arranged to spell her name. Another showed a bundle of yellow No. 2 pencils, each embossed with her name.

I was struck by the way this organization used the simplicity of a calendar to market its branding messages while incorporating the member's name in big, bold letters throughout.

Welcome to the new world of personalization—one of the fastest-growing trends in corporate and nonprofit marketing.

For higher education philanthropy or advancement communications, personalization is one of the best opportunities we have to engage our donors. Just as Amazon and Netflix have personalized the user experience, we too must develop personalized communication and marketing experiences.

Web and digital

According to Adobe's 2017 Digital Marketing Study, 62 percent of organizations are using automated personalization for the web. This is up a whopping 51 percent since 2016. And for mobile, the growth is even more profound. Fifty-six percent of organizations are using automated personalization for mobile—up 115 percent since 2016.

Increasingly, these constituents will look for personalized experiences when visiting our philanthropy and alumni websites. The more personal the messaging and images, the greater the opportunity we have to drive alumni engagement and philanthropic support.

Obviously, to improve website personalization strategies we must better mine the analytical data of our website users. This allows the philanthropy, alumni and advancement offices to better tailor messages to users.

Website personalization can lead to greater

online giving. Also, various CRM programs—
when connected with a website—can aid with
personalization as the once anonymous visitor
becomes an identified, named person.

Video

Institutions can offer personal attention to
constituents by integrating video on multiple
channels including social media and stand-alone
productions. Both quantitative and qualitative
research have shown that personalized video is an
effective means of reaching specific audiences.

In personalized video, viewer details such as
names and class year are incorporated in scenes
automatically and at scale. In a recent personalized
campaign, one university's advancement
department experienced more than a 70 percent
click-through-to-open rate. The previous video
campaign without personalization had only
reached 20 percent.

Email

Email as a marketing tool is making a strong

comeback with personalization.

Besides simply adding an individual's name to the communication, successful email marketing campaigns take personalization to a higher level by sending birthday and anniversary shout-outs, announcements about specially discounted ticket offers, news about important capital campaign gifts and developments, or special messaging for alumni class or affinity groups.

Print

We now come full circle – the marriage of print and personalization. Advances in digital technology and easily accessible data now permit a world of opportunity to personalize letters, postcards, direct mail, booklets and brochures.

Colleges and universities have been moving in this direction with their print marketing publications—especially for student recruitment and donor communications.

Recently over coffee, a colleague of mine said: "People will just naturally come to expect their communication from us (higher education/nonprofits) to be personalized and not even give it a second thought." She's right!

For those of us who serve our colleges, universities or nonprofit organizations in a public relations or marketing capacity, we have no other alternative but to be ready for this exciting, yet challenging, communications opportunity.

No doubt Bob Dylan would agree – "For the times they are a-changin'." Are you ready?

(An updated and expanded version of a story originally published in *University Business*. Used by permission.)

217

"

No matter how old you are or how long you've been in a communication-related field, maintain the fire in your belly. Doing so will give you the edge you need to create and perform at your finest.

"

Regardless of your title or position, lead from where you are.

"

"

In Public Relations, the
professional must lead with a
servant's heart.

"

DEVELOPING A COHESIVE EARNED MEDIA STRATEGY FOR YOUR CAPITAL CAMPAIGN

TARGET THE RIGHT NEWS OUTLETS, ENGAGE WITH THEM OVER THE LONG-TERM, AND TRACK RESULTS FOR SUCCESS

It's thrilling to be associated with an institution when a capital campaign is launched. The campus environment becomes electrified. Capital campaigns spark enthusiasm among the academic community and rally supporters, both on and off campus, as they engage with an effort that can be transformational for the institution.

But as a public relations officer, your work is about to begin. You must capture and sustain the interest of downsized news organizations so they cover the campaign and the stories behind those who are making or experiencing its philanthropic impact.

The days of distributing countless press releases to newsrooms, hoping that one might spark interest, are long gone. That equates to throwing a handful of seeds on a field of rocks and hoping that one germinates.

Today's earned media efforts demand public relations professionals to equip their PR toolboxes with strategic communication tools that include research and targeted planning, execution and measurement. Having a clear understanding of the news organization's audience and its reporters' beat interests are not only important – they're vital.

Public relations officers are often faced with a bit of a conundrum. We each recognize the tremendous challenge to keep the campaign momentum going while knowing that reporters and writers are now constantly faced with covering multiple beats – making the demands on their days even shorter, including the time they might have for you and your news pitch.

This is where an "earned media" strategy for your capital campaign comes into play. Whether you are preparing for a campaign or are already in the midst of one, it is never too late to construct and implement an earned media strategy. These are a few ways that can help you have a firmer footing on an everchanging media landscape.

Here are five ways for you to get into the ever-changing earned media landscape:

Engage with those who already know you

Start at news organizations with staffers who are already aware of and interested in your institution and its capital campaign. I'm a firm believer in the effectiveness of meeting face to face with publishers, editors, news directors, reporters and writers. These meetings can be invaluable for your institution. Introductory meetings personalize the campaign and allow you to present its scope and potential impact on the community or state. Follow-up meetings should include your president or senior leadership. Present demographic data that will localize the campaign for news organizations, such as the number of alumni and students who live in that specific area.

Cast a wide net, but have a target in mind

When I was a boy, helicopters would occasionally drop leaflets announcing store openings, church revivals, pizza delivery deals or concerts. Advertisers hoped that someone would notice and become engaged in whatever was being promoted. But we cannot afford to drop multiple press releases on unsuspecting reporters and writers hoping that one of them will notice us. We must target our messaging and identify national news organization staffers and influential bloggers who are more likely to show an interest or curiosity in how the capital campaign will help shape and transform the lives of students, faculty and researchers.

Think long term

As most of us appreciate, effective media relations is not a one-and-done deal. You must always consider your next steps. What will follow your face-to-face conversation, email, phone call, editorial board meeting or pitch? After all, public relations is about relationship building and can result in meaningful, productive interactions with editors, news directors, writers and reporters.

Understand the power of the pitch

Most media staffers prefer concise emails that pique their curiosity. However, some prefer a phone call or text. Also, make sure your capital campaign-related pitch is timely, relevant and relatable to the news organization's audience.

Measure your effectiveness

Measuring an earned media strategy has become much more sophisticated and analytically-driven in recent years. Software measurement tools are now available that will allow public relations professionals to monitor true reach versus potential reach of a published or reported story. Using capital campaign-tracking URLs and campaign-specific hashtags in your news releases are other excellent ways to monitor the effectiveness of your efforts.

(An updated and expanded version of a story originally published in *University Business*. Used by permission.)

"

Hundreds of people just as bright and talented as you would love to be seated where you are. Be grateful each day for the opportunity to serve where you are.

"

"

Young professional: Cherish the wealth of knowledge and wisdom senior professionals bring and learn from them.

"

Senior professional: Cherish the wealth of energy and new ideas young professionals bring and learn from them.

"

REACHING COLLEGE ALUMNI, DONORS AND PARENTS THROUGH EFFECTIVE STORYTELLING

PHILANTHROPY MARKETING MEANS CONNECTING WITH A DIFFERENT AUDIENCE THAN STUDENTS

My grandfather was a master storyteller. He had an exceptional ability to engage those around him with his stories, seasoned by years of wisdom, challenge and humor.

A regular customer of his gas station once said he'd drive around town until his gas tank was nearly empty just so he could come by for one of my grandfather's stories.

Regardless if the person was a child or an adult,

my grandfather always knew his audience well. When sharing with his family, friends or customers, my granddad would capture his audience's attention by telling stories that related to them.

He never talked over the heads of people. He found common ground where people could best relate to what he was telling.

His stories would often be laced with true-to-life humor, or life challenges that were conquered by sheer will and determination—or simply messages of encouragement.

Focus on content

Those of us in higher education and in the nonprofit sector could certainly take a chapter from my grandfather's book on effective storytelling. We all know the importance of effective storytelling, yet we often fall prey to telling stories that we want to tell instead of what our audiences desire to read or hear.

This is especially true when preparing stories for

older audiences—alumni, donors and parents. Their life goals are different from those of the college-bound. They're seeking sincere, tangible ways to engage with our institutions.

To improve your storytelling, ask yourself these content questions:

- Does your story know its audience? Such a question may seem obvious, but it is imperative you prepare content for your intended audience. This must be the first question you ask yourself honestly when preparing content for your alumni, donors and parents. All too often we try to make the content prepared for student recruiting also fit our needs for reaching older audiences. As with each stage of life, our personal interests and goals change. The content we prepare should mirror that fact.

- Is your story impactful? Does the story and its supporting visuals spark an emotional connection for the reader, viewer or listener? It is critical that alumni, donors and parents relate to our stories' champions and learn how they too, in some way, can become champions for the institution.

- Does your story support the goals and objectives of the strategic plan and capital campaign? One of the best ways to develop a story idea is to link its relationship with the institution's strategic plan or, if applicable, the capital campaign. Philanthropy feature stories are among the finest ways to communicate how the fervent passion and dreams of the donor resulted in achieving an institutional priority.

- Does the story encourage others to take action? An effective story must encourage your institution's supporters to take some form of action—as a volunteer, advocate or donor. Be careful not to talk at, but rather with, your audience. Clearly present ways your alumni, donors and parents can become engaged in the life of your institution, then offer them excellent examples of those whose philanthropic leadership is paving the way. This will challenge and inspire them to become involved, too.

The pay-off

Test your content with a small sampling of alumni, donors and parents. Allow them to provide feedback on the stories you prepare. One-on-one meetings—rather than electronic surveys or focus groups—will provide you with keen, personalized insights for improved story-telling.

This approach takes time but, in the long run, it will pay off in a big way for your communication shop.

Examine opportunities to blend photography and video with written online content. Not only will this satisfy your audience's information needs, it will greatly advance your institution's capacity for sharing its many success stories with your greatest advocates through print and digital means.

(An updated and expanded version of a story originally published in *University Business*. Used by permission.)

"

Before launching an idea, ask yourself: 'Why does this matter?' 'Does this support our organization's mission?'

"

"

Avoid humorous social media posts. What might seem hilarious to you might be insulting for someone else. Be smart and play it safe.

"

"

When others tell you, 'We've tried that before and it didn't work,' think how you might retool that idea to make it incredibly successful!

"

Fundraising ideas: Donor relations in the digital age

Most people use social media these days, so fundraisers should, too

Few of us would be surprised to learn that young adults have been the earliest adopters of social media. However, don't be fooled into thinking that older adults, particularly baby boomers, are not active users.

In a 2017 study conducted by the Pew Research Center, nearly 7 in 10 Americans reported using social media "to connect with one another, engage with news content, share information and entertain themselves." And use by older adults has increased in recent years—catapulting from only 3 percent in 2006 to nearly 70 percent in 2016.

What does this data tell those of us in the higher education philanthropy profession? Our supporters are communicating with one another and their friends through social media. It is therefore incumbent on us to become active in the digital conversation.

Reaching your most valued audience

Don't think that social media is not important—even if you don't personally use it. Social media is a vital, measurable aspect of donor cultivation, donor relations, stewardship and philanthropy communications.

Data supports that our key audiences are actively engaged—especially with Facebook. The platform's largest user group is the 35 to 54 age range, with the 55-plus market growing at lightning speed. In fact, some surveys find that more than 80 percent of baby boomers are now using social media. Consider how your marketing strategies might reach this demographic via Facebook.

As for millennials (ages 18 to 29), more than 90 percent are using social media and mobile apps. Consider how your annual giving and crowdfunding marketing strategies can engage this group of users.

Beyond Facebook

Social media is also a critical communications tool for expanding a capital campaign's branding awareness, audience reach, messaging and donor engagement. In addition, colleges and universities should include social networking strategies in major gift programs.

For example, LinkedIn provides a wealth of opportunities and data mining for alumni engagement, donor research, relationship building, networking and donor cultivation. Donors and prospects want to know if your organization is trustworthy, how it's impacting the world, and how they can become involved financially and as volunteers.

Social media provides ease of access to your

institution and the communication tools they must have to become even more effective advocates for your cause.

As you prepare your social media strategies, consider the following tips:

- Be authentic in your social media messaging. After all, your institution is competing virtually with other colleges, universities and nonprofits worldwide. Social media messaging should be focused on what your donors want—not necessarily what you believe is most important.

- Know that social media generates word-of-mouth support for your cause and can strengthen donor loyalty.

- Be strategic in your institution's posts. Messaging should inform, inspire and engage.

- Realize social media's "live" features will expand. Be smart, strategic and professional in their use. Think like a journalist as you implement in-the-moment features.

- Continually update content with fresh, relevant and engaging information. Even a wonderful loaf of freshly baked bread will grow stale if kept on the shelf too long.

- Repurpose your best content—including outstanding story profiles, thought leadership quotes, video clips and photos.

- In social media efforts, point followers back to the institution or philanthropy office's website and vice versa.

- Use no more than one to three social media platforms and do them well.

- Face-to-face interaction will always be the most important and preferred approach to major and principal gift solicitation. Social media, however, can help open the door.

(An updated and expanded version of a story originally published in *University Business*. Used by permission.)

"

Don't forget to have fun along the way. Enjoy the journey!

"

"

Drink coffee. And plenty of it.

"

"

Before a news conference, always brush and floss your teeth and make sure your zipper's zipped and buttons buttoned. Just saying…

"

MAKING MEMORIES ON CAMPUS

MAXIMIZING THE RELATIONAL AND MARKETING BENEFITS OF ALUMNI AND PHILANTHROPIC EVENTS

Most of us in higher education enjoy planning for and attending special events. From formal occasions to casual functions, colleges and universities have long hosted events as a means of engaging alumni, parents and families, donors, and other valued supporters.

Designated weekends, such as homecoming, parents weekend and alumni weekend, also provide meaningful occasions to invite members of the family "back home."

For alumni, events can rekindle memories of

student days and encourage reconnections with friends, faculty and student organizations.

For parents, events can strengthen their relationship with their child while instilling a sense of pride in their child's chosen academic home.

And for other supporters such as donors, events can stir passion, belief and confirmation in the worthy cause for which they invest their time, creativity, advocacy and personal resources.

Strategic planning

Events can be one of the most effective public relations, fundraising and marketing efforts an institution can undertake. Too often, however, institutions overlook the strategic opportunities events can present. The following aspects of event planning can catapult your event from tactical to strategic success.

Have a clear vision

Make certain there is an overall vision and mission for the event, and stay true to that goal throughout planning. What is the event's intended outcome? How can this achieve your institution's overall fundraising and public relations strategies? What will be the follow-up with your guests? How can they relive parts of the event should they wish to share their memories with family, friends and business associates?

Be exceptional

See to the smallest details and help your guests make memories. Your guests will remember that extra touch and will continue to support you in the future. Strive to create events that will provide memorable moments that will leave an indelible impression on hearts and minds.

Plan with the five basic human senses in mind

With an event, you want to plan around hearing, sight, smell, taste and touch. As you explore ideas, consider how one or more of these senses can add to the memorability of your event.

Know your guests and motivate them to action

Do a deep dive into understanding who your guests are, including their likes and dislikes, interests in your institution, and possible connections with your college or university. In agricultural terms, you're planting seeds for further growth. Don't allow something special to become a "one and done." Build on what you've started.

Plan for your audience

Programming, entertainment, food and swag are vital considerations for the audience you wish to attract. Pay attention to the details for each as they are critical components of your event. Provide a setting that is comfortable for your guests, yet sparkles with out-of-the-ordinary treats such as valet parking and students welcoming guests at doorways.

Emotionally engage your audience

Find an appropriate way for your audience to become emotionally engaged in your event's program. Storytelling and personal testimonials resonate with all of us and can effectively advance our worthy cause with an audience eager to learn more.

In their book, *The Power of Moments*, authors Chip and Dan Heath write: "Moments matter. And what an opportunity we miss when we leave them to chance! Teachers can inspire, caregivers can comfort, service workers can delight, politicians can unite and managers can motivate. All it takes is a bit of insight and forethought."

And so it goes for event planning, too. With some insight and forethought, you can create events that produce powerful, engaging moments for your guests.

(An updated and expanded version of a story originally published in *University Business*. Used by permission.)

"

Every person in your organization matters. As members of a symphony orchestra, we each have critical roles to play in our organization's success as we perform in perfect harmony.

"

"

Get to know strangers. All too often, we stay within our own circle of friends without straying too far to engage with others who are not like us.

"

"

A brand is built and maintained
by your reputation and how well
you fulfill what you promise,
not the institution or
organization's logo and tagline.

"

"

Never assume your internal audience understands the work that you do. Internal communication is critical.

Concluding Thoughts

The Signature of Your Work

The importance of everyone's role recently struck me as I watched from my office window a stonemason skillfully and artfully cut and chisel stones that have since become part of several new, handsomely designed stone walls in a plaza on the University of Kentucky campus.

As I watched, I was captivated by the stonemason's unfailing devotion to the project's final achievement. I marveled from a distance at his attention to detail. He seemed to know where each stone should instinctively go as he placed the gray limestone blocks with expert care and confidence.

Even though his signature will never appear

chiseled on any of the stones or engraved on a bronze plaque recognizing his name, this craftsman's passion for the work will stand the test of time.

For him, his work *was* his signature – his calling.

Others who casually pass by these walls or sit on them while conversing with friends and colleagues will never know this man's name or appreciate the hours of sweat, muscle, skill, eye to detail and patience it took for him to accomplish his masterpiece. But *he* will.

Watching this stonemason perform his duties was a beautiful reminder that no job is too big or too small and that all of us, no matter our title or responsibilities, can help build and shape an affirming, can-do work environment that is purposeful, meaningful and electric, and like these stone walls, built to withstand whatever form of weather that comes that day.

Your *signature* on the work you execute represents, like that stonemason's, your *reputation* and *credibility* as a public relations and marketing professional. And that is true any time you craft messages in response to crises; strategically position thought leadership before targeted audiences; execute and manage your brand; purposefully place op-eds; cultivate honest and productive relations with members of the media; create ads, photographs or publications; write news releases or pitch stories; organize and manage a speakers bureau; stand before audiences while representing your institution or organization; thoughtfully post social media content; attend any meeting; host and record podcasts; lay out magazine pages; coordinate special events and news conferences; or perform "all other duties as assigned."

Few will ever know or appreciate the hours it took to accomplish those successful efforts — but you will. After all, genuine efforts in our profession are not about the "me," but on the "we."

Never allow yourself to slip into giving just the

minimal effort. Give it your all! Your signature work should always strive to be your finest masterpieces.

Everyone has an important role to play — including you. Our profession needs you. We need your heart, your passion and your desire to make a difference.

I know you will succeed!

BIBLIOGRAPHY

Beckwith, Harry. *Selling the Invisible: A Field Guide to Modern Marketing.* New York: Business Plus, 1997.

Bolton, Roger. (Nov. 6, 2019) "The Power of Diversity, Civility and Authenticity." The 20th James C. Bowling Executive-in-Residence Lecture, University of Kentucky. Retrieved from https://ci.uky.edu/isc/power-diversity-civility-and-authenticity-roger-bolton-president-page

Clifford, Christine. *Let's Close A Deal: Turn Contacts into Paying Customers for Your Company, Product, Service or Cause.* Hoboken, New Jersey: John Wiley & Sons, 2013.

Fox, Michael. *Town & Gown: From Conflict to Cooperation*. Union, Ontario: Municipal World Inc., 2014.

Fry, Igielnik and Patten. (March 16, 2018) "How Millennials today compare with their grandparents 50 years ago," Pew Research Center. Retrieved from https://www.pewresearch.org/fact-tank/2018/03/16/how-millennials-compare-with-their-grandparents/.

Hazlett, Kirk. (October 30, 2013). "PR 'Professional' or 'Practitioner." *Deirdre Breakenridge 'PR Expanded.'* Retrieved from https://www.deirdrebreakenridge.com/pr-professional-or-practitioner/.

Heath, Chip and Heath, Dan. *The Power of Moments*. New York: Simon & Schuster, 2017.

Solis, Brian and Breakenridge, Deirdre. *Putting the Public Back in Public Relations: How Social Media Is Reinventing the Aging Business of PR*. Upper Saddle River, New Jersey: Pearson Education, 2009.

U.S. Travel Association Fact Sheet. (March 2019). Retrieved from https://www.ustravel.org/system/files/media_root/document/Research_Fact-Sheet_US-Travel-Answer-Sheet.pdf

Hi, Friend!

Thank you for joining me through the pages of this book. I hope in some small way something was written that might encourage, support, inform or guide you on your way in our profession —whether you serve in public relations, marketing or both.

We are certainly blessed to advance our institution or organization through the role that we lead. Don't underestimate the value your role brings.

At times, your position may be stressful. Many more times you'll be thrilled to be a part of memory-making moments that were well-executed ideas or strategies undertaken by you and your team.

Throughout your career journey, always find the joy of serving others. There's nothing better!

I would enjoy hearing from you. Let's connect on LinkedIn (www.linkedin.com/in/marcwhitt/) and Twitter (@marcwhitt). Or if you like, you may simply email me at marcuscwhitt@gmail.com.

I wish you all the very best as you continue to make a lasting difference in our world.

-Marc

Galatians 6:9

ABOUT THE AUTHOR

Marc Whitt is Director of Media & Strategic Relations at the University of Kentucky's Office of Public Relations and Strategic Communications. He also serves as a part-time instructor in UK's Department of Integrated Strategic Communication and is a former PR and marketing columnist for the national trade magazine, *University Business.*

During his more than 30 years in higher education, Marc's work has achieved measurable results garnering over 40 honors including back-to-back CASE Silver Medal Awards for Total Institutional Relations Program. In 2015, he received the James C. Bowling Excellence in Public Relations Award. Presented by the UK Journalism Alumni Association and UK Department of Integrated Strategic Communication, the award is given to the "outstanding public relations professional with ties to Kentucky." That same year, he received the Distinguished Alumnus Award from the Eastern Kentucky University Department of Communication.

Recently Onalytica, a firm that identifies social influencers, named him among the "Top 100 Public Relations Influencers on Twitter;" he was ranked 21st. Additionally, CASE Kentucky presented him with its Beth K. Fields Service Award for Leadership in Advancement.

In previous years, Marc has served on the Association of American Colleges & Universities Advisory Council on Communications and Public Affairs (two of his eight years as national chair), the CASE District III (Southeast US) Board of Directors and the International Town & Gown Association Board of Directors.

A trumpet player, Marc is a native of Paintsville, Kentucky. He and his wife, Jennifer, reside in Richmond, Kentucky, and are the parents of Emily Fields (Mark), Elizabeth Muncie (Christian) and Jacob; and the grandparents of Annaleigh and Aubrey Fields.

Made in the USA
Monee, IL
23 September 2021